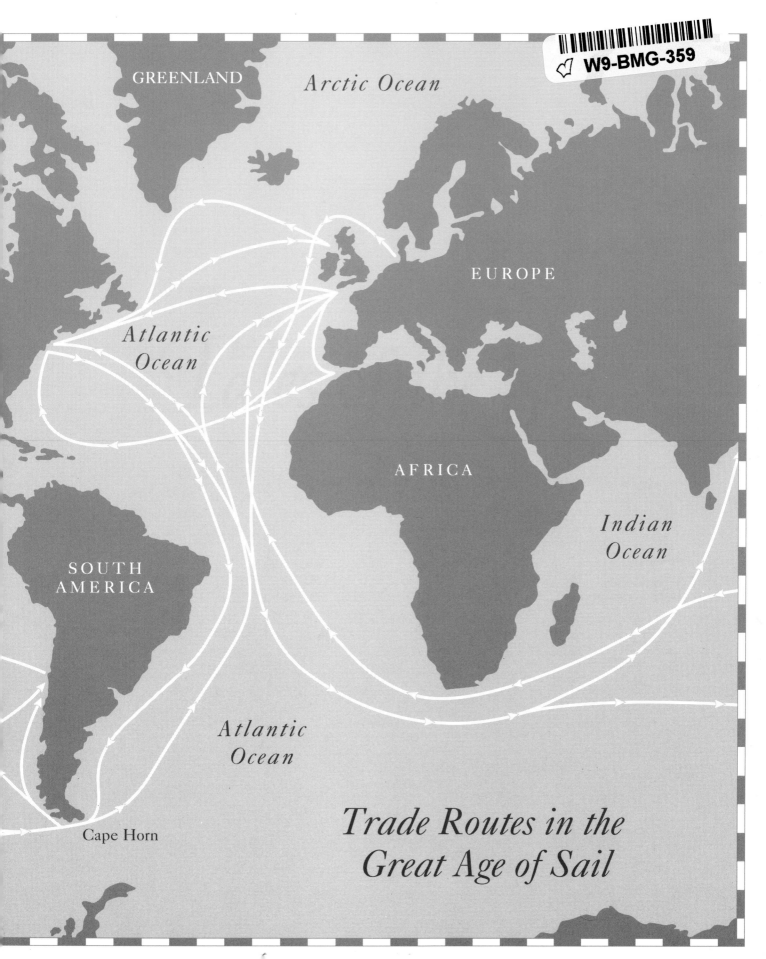

GREENLAND

Arctic Ocean

EUROPE

Atlantic Ocean

AFRICA

SOUTH AMERICA

Indian Ocean

Atlantic Ocean

Cape Horn

Trade Routes in the Great Age of Sail

An Illustrated Collection of Adventure Stories

Tales of the Sea

South Street Seaport Museum

RIZZOLI
NEW YORK

First published in the United States of America in 1992 by
Rizzoli International Publications, Inc.
300 Park Avenue South, New York, New York 10010

Printed and bound in Singapore

Library of Congress Cataloging-in-Publication Data
Tales of the Sea: an illlustrated collection of Adventure stories
Introduction by Frank V. Snyder: preface by Peter Neill
p.   cm.
Summary: A collection of sea stories by such authors as
Herman Melville, Wilkie Collins and Thor Heyerdahl.
ISBN 0-8478-1578-1
1. Sea stories 2. Children's stories [1. Sea stories 2. Short
stories.] I. South Street Seaport Museum (New York, N.Y.)
PZ5. T265   1992
[Fic]—dc   2092-2841
                    CIP   AC

For Rizzoli:
Lois Brown and Isabelle Bleecker

For the South Street Seaport Museum:
Norman Bower, Charles Sachs, and Sally Yerkovich

Design: Pamela Fogg
Design Assistant: Betty Lew

Contents

Introduction

The Great Age of Sail, as historians call it, began in the 1850s when the first clipper ships appeared on the high seas. It was a period marked by enormous advances in sailing ship design, culminating in the huge steel "windjammers" that could easily move at 18 to 20 knots fully loaded, and that often rolled up day's runs of 350 miles or more. It was during this period that most of the sea tales in this book were written.

As we now know, rapid as were the advances in square rigger design, the development of the steamship was even faster, so that, by 1900, the smoky, dirty steamer was replacing the lovely and romantic wind-driven ship. Almost a hundred years after it had begun, the Great Age of Sail came to a sad ending with the outbreak of World War II. All the remaining steel windjammers ended up in wreckers' yards, with only three or four saved by maritime museums and a few more retrieved as sail training ships.

But, just as these giant wind ships were disappearing from the oceans, a curious thing was happening: sailing was rapidly expanding as a sport for the common man. In its early days, recreational sailing was called "yachting," and most of the sailing organizations were called "yacht clubs." The New York Yacht Club, formed in 1844, was one of the first. Today, there are well over a thousand such clubs in the United States alone, and the number of recreational sailors has grown into the millions.

One of the great contributions that the yacht clubs have made over the years has been the creation of junior clubs whose purpose has been primarily to teach youngsters seamanship and racing tactics. I was an early beneficiary of one of these programs, way back in the mid-1930s; here I learned the basics at an early age—a wonderful opportunity that was not offered at many clubs then, but which has since become common.

Another development that has helped put young people on the water has been the design of safe, small boats. By all odds, the most successful and popular of the thousands of small sailboats that have appeared in the last fifty years is also just about the smallest and safest. This is an eight-foot-long pram with the delightful name of the Optimist Dinghy. The Optimist is built of fiberglass, has a squared-off bow and stern, buoyancy tanks, and a tiny mast and sail. It can easily be handled by one person, even a small child, and is amazingly fast and maneuverable. It is always raced single-handed, and almost always by kids.

Today, there are a million Optimists sailing here and abroad—yes, one million. Over half of them are enrolled in organized club fleets. Every year, regional, national, and international regattas are held, to which young competitors flock from all over the world. There are plenty of eight- to fourteen-year-olds out there who handle these boats like the experts they are. I've seen them do it! But, by the time these young sailors have reached fifteen years of age, they no longer qualify to race in the Optimist events and so must move up to larger boats.

Larger boats present no problem at all. For those who live far from the water and who want to transport their craft easily, there are the phenomenally successful "car-top" boats: the Sailfish, Sunfish, and Laser. Over a hundred thousand of each of these have been built. The most successful of this kind of splinter-boat is the "sail board," which was first introduced only twenty years ago. Today, sail boards are among the fastest and most popular of all sailing craft. They easily reach speeds of 20 knots in fresh breezes.

For those who like speed but prefer to stay a little bit drier, there are dozens of planing centerboarder designs—to name only four: the International 14, Flying Fifteen, Finn, and Flying Dutchman, all of which have been or still are Olympic classes. I have owned a boat like this for many years and can testify that it is thrilling, when you break out into a plane and instantly accelerate to 14 knots.

Then, there are those conservative types who like the feeling of a lead-ballasted keel under them. There are another hundred or so "one design" classes for them that can be seen racing in just about every harbor, sound, and lake in the country, boats like the venerable Star, the Herreshoff S, the Atlantic, Soling, Etchells 22, and J-24.

All of this is grand fun and great sport, but, to me, the ultimate sailing adventure is going to sea in a big, well-found sailing vessel. I've done it for about fifty years now. This is where the sea tests your seamanship and staying power; this is where you encounter nature in the raw, where the going can be tough.

Running between New York and Bermuda is the Gulf Stream, that hot river in the sea which can cook up a force-12 storm in three hours, sometimes with little or no warning from our national weather service. Popular writers have concocted a wonderful myth, which they have entitled "the Bermuda Triangle" and which endows this piece of ocean with mysterious, even occult, powers that cause radios to malfunction and compasses to go in circles. What nonsense! True, the waters in and around the Gulf Stream are very dangerous at times, but not because of some obscure radio or magnetic emanation. The danger exists simply because of the incredible power of two primeval forces—wind and water.

I submit that it is incorrect to describe the sea as treacherous, cruel, or malignant, or by any other such adjective that implies an intelligence, demonic or otherwise. No, the sea is simply an enormous, inanimate liquid body, usually limpid and serene, but which can be readily and quickly stirred up to terrifying heights by gale winds.

It is when winds reach hurricane force of 70 knots or more that waves will build in height from twenty to sixty feet and will move forward at speeds of 20 knots or more. What makes these waves so dangerous is the upper section, which often breaks into massive white water that jets down the forward slope of the wave with terrific force. The impact on your little ship is something like being hit by a trailer truck every fifteen seconds or so. Indeed, when hurricane force winds drive against the Gulf Stream's 4-knot current, the seas can be frightful, and not even the strongest and largest ship is safe. That is the true significance of the name "Bermuda Triangle."

Nevertheless, properly designed small offshore sailboats are meant to take such a licking and to survive. I have experienced three such storms in the Gulf Stream in three different boats, and, each time, we came through with very little damage. Yes, the sea can be a terrific and awe-inspiring force, but a good boat, properly handled, will bring you through.

When you read these wonderful stories, remember this: going forth on the sea on a sailing craft is one of the most glorious of all adventures, for, while the sea is demanding and dangerous at times, it is also a grand taskmaster. It will repay your efforts with great beauty, with exhilaration, and, perhaps most important of all, with a wonderful sense of accomplishment.

Commodore Frank V. Snyder,
New York Yacht Club

A former Commodore of the New York Yacht Club, Frank V. Snyder has competed in numerous ocean races, and has recently completed an eleven-thousand-mile voyage from the East Coast of the United States, through the Panama Canal, and across the South Pacific to New Zealand.

Preface

You have been drawn to this marvelous collection of tales, no doubt, by an idea of the sea—the romance and mystery and high adventure that are traditionally associated with voyages of exploration. And it is true that we have been drawn to sea life for all time by such powerful, ephemeral notions, notions that have lured us away from safe and sedentary havens toward uncertainty and danger "before the mast."

Your expectations will be met here. These stories depict heroic adventures and appeal to our imagination. They take place on the surface of a tumultuous ocean and the surface of our senses. We feel the disorienting darkness of midnight; we hear the looming power of the wave; we see the windmarks on the water like scars on the writer's soul. The sea can be such a vivid, exhilarating place—especially when, secure in our reading chairs, we are neither at risk nor accountable.

But, in reality, whether caught in the "doldrums" or "in a blow," life at sea is *hard*. Hard a-lee. Hardtack. Hard aground. A ship is a hard school where every member of the crew is both teacher and pupil. There is a strong tradition of apprenticeship at sea. The newest lad aboard learns through his every watch and from his every mate. Even the captain, the *master* as he is often called, however old a sea dog he may be, learns each day—and the wrecks scattered on the rocks and reefs off every shore bear witness to the telling lesson that he may not ever learn enough.

Sons follow fathers in this business, and get their wisdom by working with their hands. Sometimes they work apart; most times they work together to hoist, to haul, to furl, to counter the force of wind and water through their collective knowledge and will. Beyond strong backs or blocks and tackles, their leverage is experience. A seaman is respected not for what he shouts or shows, but for what he does and knows.

Joshua Slocum was an uncommon sailor because he made his voyages alone. Most of us don't; we sail in consort with members of a crew, a community with all its social distinctions and human prejudices confined aboard. There is nowhere to run, no space in which to hide. Historically, crews are drawn from diverse race, class, and nation with every inclination to conflict. But the sea is a great equalizer, and its indifference to color of skin, birthright, and patriotism is well demonstrated. Rank aboard ship is by order of function and responsibility, authority is central, and contention is mitigated by discipline, order, and routine. It is an efficient political system, and, while certainly not democratic, it typically results in a crew whose personal eccentricities are conformed to the personality of the ship, and in a ship whose voyage is completed through the cooperative competence of the crew.

It transcends formal education. Indeed, these people must be very good at what they do. They always must be right; they must tie the knot that holds; they must guide themselves by sun and stars; they must know. And they must do all this in a seascape of constant change where things are never the same twice, where just beyond the horizon moves new weather and more treacherous water, where, within them, terror can suddenly rise to transform them into victims. Sailors must navigate, not just through the longitude and latitude of the specific passage, but through life. They must see things clearly; they must decide; they must place themselves accurately; they must live among themselves peacefully for long periods of time and stress; they must make their personal landfall safely through impenetrable fog.

Many of these accounts tell of solitude at sea, solitude as distinct from loneliness. In effect, the sea is wilderness, a place apart, characterized by all the dynamism and beauty of nature. As a result, it becomes a frequent context for self-realization, for growth and the coming of age, for recognition of change. People go to sea to find themselves, and do so in an atmosphere of movement, sensation, and light. The exhilaration of their response finds its way into our shoreside language and accounts for much metaphor, poetry, and art. The stories of this anthology—and their illustrative prints, paintings, and models—are only a suggestion of the full spectrum of their discovery.

This is a vast patrimony. The maritime contribution to the culture and commerce of our nation is enormous, and yet we are remarkably ignorant of it. The lessons of history do not seem to penetrate our contemporary state of mind very well and that is a great tragedy. "The sea connects all things;" its universality touches us, every one, and thus I submit that what it can teach is essential to the definition of values commensurate with the challenges we face as we embark on whatever our personal voyage. Whoever you may be, dear reader, find a way to go to sea!

Peter Neill,
President, South Street Seaport Museum

True Stories of
Adventure

Journal of the First Voyage of Columbus

Columbus' Introduction:

Because, O most Christian, and very high, very excellent and puissant Princes, King and Queen of the Spains and of the islands of the Sea, our Lords, in this present year of 1492, acting on the information that I had given to your Highnesses touching the lands of India, resolved to send me, Cristobal Colon, to the said parts of India, and ordered that I should not go by land to the eastward, but by way of the west, whither up to this day we do not know for certain that anyone has gone.

Thus, in the month of January, your Highnesses gave orders to me that with a sufficient fleet I should go to the said parts of India, and for this they made great concessions to me, and ennobled me, so that henceforward I should be called *Don*, and should be chief Admiral of the Ocean Sea, perpetual Viceroy and Governor of all the islands and continents that I should discover and gain and that I might hereafter discover and gain in the Ocean Sea, and that my eldest son should succeed, and so on from generation to generation for ever.

I left the city of Granada on the 12th of May, in the same year of 1492, being Saturday,

and came to the town of Palos which is a seaport; where I equipped three vessels well suited for such service and departed from that port, well supplied with provisions and with many sailors, on the 3rd day of August of the same year, being Friday, half an hour before sunrise, taking the route to the islands of Canaria, belonging to your Highnesses, which are in the said Ocean Sea, that I might thence take my departure for navigating until I should arrive at the Indies. As part of my duty I thought it well to write an account of all the voyage very punctually, noting from day to day all that I should do and see, that should happen, as will be seen further on. Also, Lords Princes, I resolved to describe each night what passed in the day, and to note each day how I navigated at night. I propose to construct a new chart for navigating, on which I shall delineate all the sea and lands of the Ocean in their proper positions under their bearings; and further, I propose to prepare a book, and to put down all as it were in a picture, by latitude from the equator, and western longitude. Above all, I shall have accomplished much, for I shall forget sleep, and shall work at the business of navigation, that so the service may be performed; all which will entail great labor.

WOODCUT OF COLUMBUS' FIRST VOYAGE

From *The Journal:*

Wednesday, 10th of October

The course was WSW, and they went at the rate of ten miles an hour, occasionally twelve miles, and sometimes seven. During the day and night they made fifty-nine leagues, counted as no more than forty-four. Here the people could endure no longer. They complained of the length of the voyage. But the Admiral cheered them up in the best way he could, giving them good hopes of the advantages they might gain from it. He added that, however much they might complain, he had to go to the Indies, and that he would go on until he found them, with the help of our Lord.

Thursday, 11th of October

The course was WSW, and there was more sea than there had been during the whole of the voyage. They saw sandpipers, and a green reed near the ship. Those of the caravel *Pinta* saw a cane and a pole, and they took up another small pole which appeared to have been worked with iron; also another bit of cane, a land-plant, and a small board. The crew of the caravel *Nina* also saw signs of land, and a small branch covered with berries. Everyone breathed afresh and rejoiced at these signs. The run until sunset was twenty-seven leagues.

After sunset the Admiral returned to his original west course, and they went along at the rate of twelve miles an hour. Up to two hours after midnight they had gone ninety miles, equal to twenty-two and a half

WOODCUT OF CARAVEL SIMILAR TO SANTA MARIA

land was close. When they said the *Salve*, which all the sailors were accustomed to sing in their way, the Admiral asked and admonished the men to keep a good lookout on the forecastle, and to watch well for land; and to him who should first cry out that he saw land, he would give a silk doublet, besides the other rewards promised by the Sovereigns, which were ten thousand *maravedis* to him who should first see it. At two hours after midnight the land was sighted at a distance of two leagues. They shortened sail, and lay by under the mainsail without the bonnets. The vessels were hove to, waiting for daylight; and on Friday they arrived at a small island of the Lucayos, called, in the language of the Indians, *Guanahani*. Presently they saw naked people. The Admiral went on shore in the armed boat, and Martin Alonso Pinzón, and Vicente Yañez Pinzón, his brother, who was captain of the *Niña*. The Admiral took the royal standard, and the captains went with two banners of the green cross, which the Admiral took in all the ships as a sign, with an F and a Y and a crown over each letter, one on one side of the cross and the other on the other. Having landed, they saw trees very green, and much water, and fruits of diverse kinds. The Admiral called to the two captains, and to the others who leaped on shore, and to Rodrigo Escovedo, secretary of the whole fleet, and to Rodrigo Sánchez of Segovia, and said that they should bear faithful testimony that he, in presence of all, had taken, as he now took, possession of the said island for the King and for the Queen, his Lords making the declarations that are required, as is more largely set forth in the testimonies which were then made in writing.

Presently many inhabitants of the island assembled. What follows is in the actual words of the Admiral in his book of the first navigation and discovery of the Indies. "I," he says, "that we might form great friendship, for I knew that they were a people who could be more easily freed and converted to our holy faith by love than by force, gave to some of them red caps, and glass beads to put round their necks, and many other things of little value, which gave them great pleasure, and made them so much our friends that it was a marvel to see. They afterwards came to the ship's boats where we were, swimming and bringing us parrots, cotton threads in skeins, darts, and many other things; and we exchanged them for other things that we gave them,

leagues. As the caravel *Pinta* was a better sailer, and went ahead of the Admiral, she found the land, and made the signals ordered by the Admiral. The land was first seen by a sailor named Rodrigo de Triana. But the Admiral, at ten in the previous night, being on the castle of the poop, saw a light, though it was so uncertain that he could not affirm it was land. He called Pero Gutierrez, a gentleman of the King's bedchamber, and said that there seemed to be a light, and that he should look at it. He did so, and saw it. The Admiral said the same to Rodrigo Sánchez of Segovia, whom the King and Queen had sent with the fleet as inspector, but he could see nothing, because he was not in a place whence anything could be seen. After the Admiral had spoken he saw the light once or twice, and it was like a wax candle rising and falling. It seemed to few to be an indication of land; but the Admiral made certain that

such as glass beads and small bells. In fine, they took all, and gave what they had with good will. It appeared to me to be a race of people very poor in everything. They go as naked as when their mothers bore them, and so do the women, although I did not see more than one young girl. All I saw were youths, none more than thirty years of age. They are very well made, with very handsome bodies, and very good countenances. Their hair is short and coarse, almost like the hairs of a horse's tail. They wear the hairs brought down to the eyebrows, except a few locks behind, which they wear long and never cut. They paint themselves black, and they are the color of the Canarians, neither black nor white. Some paint themselves white, others red, and others of what color they find. Some paint their faces, others the whole body, some only round the eyes, others only on the nose. They neither carry nor know anything of arms, for I showed them swords, and they took them by the blade and cut themselves through ignorance. They have no iron, their darts being wands without iron, some of them having a fish's tooth at the end, and others being pointed in various ways. They are all of fair stature and size, with good faces, and well made. I saw some with marks of wounds on their bodies, and I made signs to ask what it was, and they gave me to understand that people from other adjacent islands came with the intention of seizing them, and that they defended themselves. I believed, and still believe, that they come here from the mainland to take them prisoners. They should be good servants and intelligent, for I observed that they quickly took in what was said to them, and I believe that they would easily be made Christians, as it appeared to me that they had no religion. I, our Lord being pleased, will take hence, at the time of my departure, six natives for your Highnesses, that they may learn to speak. I saw no beast of any kind except parrots, on this island." The above is in the words of the Admiral.

The actual log kept by Christopher Columbus (1451–1506) has never been found. But two of his contemporaries had read it and made notes. These selections—an introductory note and the 10th and 11th of October, 1492—are from the approximated diary. He made the historic landing on Watling Island in the Bahamas October 12, 1492.

Driven by a Tempest

Captain Joshua Slocum

It was the 3rd of March when the *Spray* sailed from Port Tamar direct for Cape Pillar, with the wind from the northeast, which I fervently hoped might hold till she cleared the land; but there was no such good luck in store. It soon began to rain and thicken in the northwest, boding no good. The *Spray* neared Cape Pillar rapidly, and, nothing loath, plunged into the Pacific Ocean at once, taking her first bath of it in the gathering storm. There was no turning back even had I wished to do so, for the land was now shut out by the darkness of night. The wind freshened, and I took in a third reef. The sea was confused and treacherous. In such a time as this the old fisherman prayed, "Remember, Lord, my ship is so small and thy sea is so wide!" I saw now only the gleaming crests of waves. They showed white teeth while the sloop balanced over them. "Everything for an offing," I cried, and to this end I carried on all the sail she would bear. She ran all night with a free sheet, but on the morning of March 4 the wind shifted to southwest, then back suddenly to northwest, and blew with terrific force. The *Spray*, stripped of her sails, then bore off under bare poles. No ship in the world could have stood up against so violent a gale. Knowing that this storm might continue for many days, and that it would be impossible to work back to the westward along the coast outside of Tierra del Fuego, there seemed nothing to do but to keep on and go east about, after all. Anyhow, for my present safety the only course lay in keeping her before the wind. And so she drove southeast, as though about to round the Horn, while the waves rose and fell and bellowed their never-ending story of the sea; but the hand that held these held also the *Spray*. She was running now with a reefed forestaysail, the sheets flat amidship. I paid out two long ropes to steady her course and to break combing seas astern, and I lashed the helm amidships. In this trim she ran before it, shipping never a sea. Even while the storm raged at its worst, my ship was wholesome and noble. My mind as to her seaworthiness was put to ease for aye.

When all had been done that I could do for the safety of the vessel, I got to the fore-scuttle, between seas, and prepared a pot of coffee over a wood fire, and made a good Irish stew. Then, as before and afterward on the *Spray*, I insisted on warm meals. In the tide-race off Cape Pillar, however, where the sea was marvelously high, uneven, and crooked, my appetite was slim, and for a time I postponed cooking. (Confidentially, I was seasick!)

The first day of the storm gave the *Spray* her actual test in the worst sea that

Cape Horn or its wild regions could afford, and in no part of the world could a rougher sea be found than at this particular point, namely, off Cape Pillar, the grim sentinel of the Horn.

Farther offshore, while the sea was majestic, there was less apprehension of danger. There the *Spray* rode, now like a bird on the crest of a wave, and now like a waif deep down in the hollow between seas; and so she drove on. Whole days passed, counted as other days, but with always a thrill—yes, of delight.

On the fourth day of the gale, rapidly nearing the pitch of Cape Horn, I inspected my chart and pricked off the course and distance to Port Stanley, in the Falkland Islands, where I might find my way and refit, when I saw through a rift in the clouds a high mountain, about seven leagues away on the port beam. The fierce edge of the gale by this time had blown off, and I had already bent a square sail on the boom in place of the mainsail, which was torn to rags. I hauled in the trailing ropes, hoisted this awkward sail reefed, the forestaysail being already set, and under this sail brought her at once on the wind heading for the land, which appeared as an island in the sea. So it turned out to be, though not the one I had supposed.

I was exultant over the prospect of once more entering the Strait of Magellan and beating through again into the Pacific, for it was more than rough on the outside coast of Tierra del Fuego. It was indeed a mountainous sea. When the sloop was in the fiercest squalls, with only the reefed forestaysail set, even that small sail shook her from keelson to truck when it shivered by the leech. Had I harbored the shadow of a doubt for her safety, it would have been that she might spring a leak in the garboard at the heel of the mast; but she never called me once to the pump. Under pressure of the smallest sail I could set she made for the land like a racehorse, and steering her over the crests of the waves so that she might not trip was nice work. I stood at the helm now and made the most of it.

Night closed in before the sloop reached the land, leaving her feeling the way in pitchy darkness. I saw breakers ahead before long. At this I wore ship and stood offshore, but was immediately startled by the tremendous roaring of breakers again ahead and on the lee bow. This puzzled me, for there should have been no broken water where I supposed myself to be. I kept off a good bit, then wore round, but finding broken water also there, threw her head again offshore. In this way, among dangers, I spent the rest of the night. Hail and sleet in the fierce squalls cut my flesh till the blood trickled over my face; but what of that? It was daylight, and the sloop was in the midst of the Milky Way of the sea, which is northwest of Cape Horn, and it was the white breakers of a huge sea over sunken rocks which had threatened to engulf her through the night. It was Fury Island I had sighted and steered for, and what a panorama was before me now and all around! It was not the time to complain of a broken skin. What could I do but fill away among the breakers and find a channel between them, now that it was day? Since she had escaped the rocks through the night, surely she would find her way by daylight. This was the greatest sea adventure of my life. God knows how my vessel escaped.

The sloop at last reached inside of small islands that sheltered her in smooth water. Then I climbed the mast to survey the wild scene astern. The great naturalist Darwin looked over this seascape from the deck of the *Beagle*, and wrote in his journal, "Any landsman seeing the Milky Way would have nightmare for a week." He might have added "or seaman" as well.

The *Spray's* good luck followed fast. I discovered, as she sailed along through a labyrinth of islands, that she was in the Cockburn Channel, which leads into the Strait of Magellan at a point opposite Cape Froward, and that she was already passing Thieves' Bay, suggestively named. And at night, March 8, behold, she was at anchor in a snug cove at the turn! Every heartbeat on the *Spray* now counted thanks.

Here I pondered on the events of the last few days, and, strangely enough, instead of feeling rested from sitting or lying down, I now began to feel jaded and worn; but a hot meal of venison stew soon put me right, so that I could sleep. As drowsiness came on I sprinkled the deck with tacks, and then I turned in, bearing in mind the advice of my old friend Samblich that I was not to step on them myself. I saw to it that not a few of them stood "business end" up; for when the *Spray* passed Thieves' Bay two canoes had put out and followed in her wake, and there was no disguising the fact any longer that I was alone.

Now, it is well known that one cannot step on a tack without saying something about it. A pretty good Chris-

tian will whistle when he steps on the "commercial end" of a carpet tack; a savage will howl and claw the air, and that was just what happened that night about twelve o'clock, while I was asleep in the cabin, where the savages thought they "had me," sloop and all, but changed their minds when they stepped on deck, for then they thought that I or somebody else had them. I had no need of a dog; they howled like a pack of hounds. I had hardly use for a gun. They jumped pell-mell, some into their canoes and some into the sea, to cool off, I suppose, and there was a deal of free language over it as they went. I fired several guns when I came on deck, to let the rascals know that I was home, and then I turned in again, feeling sure I should not be disturbed any more by people who left in so great a hurry.

The Fuegians, being cruel, are naturally cowards; they regard a rifle with superstitious fear. The only real danger one could see that might come from their quarter would be from allowing them to surround one within bowshot, or to anchor within range where they might lie in ambush. As for their coming on deck at night, even had I not put the tacks about, I could have cleared them off by shots from the cabin and hold. I always kept a quantity of ammunition within reach in the hold and in the cabin and in the forepeak, so that retreating to any of these places I could "hold the fort" simply by shooting up through the deck.

Perhaps the greatest danger to be apprehended was from the use of fire. Every canoe carries fire; nothing is thought of that, for it is their custom to communicate by smoke signals. The harmless brand that lies smouldering in the bottom of one of their canoes might be ablaze in one's cabin if he were not on the alert. The port captain of Sandy Point warned me particularly of this danger. Only a short time before they had fired a Chilean gunboat by throwing brands in through the stern windows of the cabin. The *Spray* had no openings in the cabin or deck, except two scuttles, and these were guarded by fastenings which could not be undone without waking me if I were asleep.

On the morning of the 9th, after a refreshing rest and a warm breakfast, and after I had swept the deck of tacks, I got out what spare canvas there was on board, and began to sew the pieces together in the shape of a peak for my square mainsail, the tarpaulin. The day to

THE SPRAY

all appearances promised fine weather and light winds, but appearances in Tierra del Fuego do not always count. While I was wondering why no trees grew on the slope abreast of the anchorage, half minded to lay by the sail making and land with my gun for some game and to inspect a white boulder on the beach, near the brook, a williwaw came down with such terrific force as to carry the *Spray*, with two anchors down, like a feather out of the cove and away into deep water. No wonder trees did not grow on the side of that hill! Great Boreas! a tree would need to be all roots to hold on against such a furious wind.

From the cove to the nearest land to leeward was a long drift, however, and I had ample time to weigh both anchors before the sloop came near any danger, and so no harm came of it. I saw no more savages that day or the next; they probably had some sign by which they knew of the coming williwaws; at least, they were wise in not being afloat even on the second day, for I had no sooner gotten to work at sail making again, after the anchor was down, than the wind, as on the day before, picked the sloop up and flung her seaward with a vengeance, anchor and all, as before. This fierce wind, usual to the Magellan country, continued on through the day, and swept the sloop by several miles of steep bluffs and precipices overhanging a bold shore of wild and uninviting appearance. I was not sorry to get away from it, though in doing so it was no Elysian shore to which I shaped my course. I kept on sailing in hope, since I had no choice but to go on, heading across for St. Nicholas Bay, where I had cast anchor February 19. It was now the 10th of March! Upon reaching the bay the second time I had circumnavigated the wildest part of desolate Tierra del Fuego. But the *Spray* had not yet arrived at St. Nicholas, and by the merest accident her bones were saved from resting there when she did arrive. The parting of a staysail-sheet in a williwaw, when the sea was turbulent and she was plunging into the storm, brought me forward to see instantly a dark cliff ahead and breakers so close under the bows that I felt surely lost, and in my thoughts cried, "Is the hand of fate against me, after all, leading me in the end to this dark spot?" I sprang aft again, unheeding the flapping sail, and threw the wheel over, expecting, as the sloop came down into the hollow of a wave, to feel her timbers smash under me on the rocks. But at the touch of her helm she swung clear of the danger, and in the next moment she was in the lee of the land.

It was the small island in the middle of the bay for which the sloop had been steering, and which she made with such unerring aim as nearly to run it down. Farther along in the bay was the anchorage, which I managed to reach, but before I could get the anchor down another squall caught the sloop and whirled her round like a top and carried her away, altogether to leeward of the bay. Still farther to leeward was a great headland, and I bore off for that. This was retracing my course toward Sandy Point, for the gale was from the southwest.

I had the sloop soon under good control, however, and in a short time rounded to under the lee of a mountain, where the sea was as smooth as a mill pond, and the sails flapped and hung limp while she carried her way close in. Here I thought I would anchor and rest till morning, the depth being eight fathoms very close to the shore. But it was interesting to see, as I let go the anchor, that it did not reach the bottom before another williwaw struck down from this mountain and carried the sloop off faster than I could pay out cable. Therefore, instead of resting, I had to "man the windlass" and heave up the anchor with fifty fathoms of cable hanging up and down in deep water. This was in that part of the strait called Famine Reach. Dismal Famine Reach! On the sloop's crab windlass I worked the rest of the night, thinking how much easier it was for me when I could say, "Do that thing or the other," than now doing all myself. But I hove away and sang the old chants that I sang when I was a sailor. Within the last few days I had passed through much and was now thankful that my state was no worse. It was daybreak when the anchor was at the hawse. By this time the wind had gone down, and cat's-paws took the place of williwaws, while the sloop drifted slowly toward Sandy Point. She came within sight of ships at anchor in the roads, and I was more than half minded to put in for new sails, but the wind coming out from the northeast, which was fair for the other direction, I turned the prow of the *Spray* westward once more for the Pacific, to traverse a second time the second half of my first course through the strait.

Born in Nova Scotia in 1844, Joshua Slocum left school at age eight and ran away from home at twelve. At sixteen he made his first ocean voyage as a seaman. Unsurpassed for sailing long distances by himself, Slocum was last seen setting out from Rhode Island on a solo voyage. This selection is from Slocum's account of sailing around the world alone in his small sloop, the Spray.

The Tireless Enemies

Sir Ernest Henry Shackleton

By midday the *James Caird* was ready for the voyage. Vincent and the carpenter had secured some dry clothes by exchange with members of the shore party, and the boat's crew was standing by, waiting for the order to cast off. I went ashore in the *Stancomb Wills* and had a last word with Wild. Secure in the knowledge that he would act wisely I told him that I trusted the party to him, and then I said "good-bye" to the men. Within a few minutes I was again aboard the *James Caird*, and the crew of the *Stancomb Wills* shook hands with us and offered us the last good wishes.

Then, setting our jib, we cut the painter and moved away to the northeast. The men who were staying behind made a pathetic little group on the beach, but they waved to us and gave three hearty cheers. There was hope in their hearts, and they trusted us to bring the help which they so sorely needed.

I had all sails set, and the *James Caird* quickly dipped the beach and its line of dark figures. The westerly wind took us rapidly to the line of pack, and as we entered it I stood up with my arm around the mast directing the steering. The pack thickened and we were forced to turn almost due east, running before the wind towards a gap which I had seen in the morning from the high ground. At 4 P.M. we found the channel, and, dropping sail, we rowed through without touching the ice, and by 5:30 P.M. we were clear of the pack with open water before us. Soon the swell became very heavy, and when it was time for our first evening meal we had great difficulty in keeping the Primus lamp alight and preventing the hoosh from splashing out of the pot.

Three men were needed to attend to the cooking, and all their operations had to be conducted in the confined space under the decking, where the men lay or knelt and adjusted themselves as best they could to the angles of our cases and ballast. It was uncomfortable, but we found consolation in the reflection that without the decking we could not have used the cooker at all.

The tale of the next sixteen days is one of supreme strife amid heaving waters, for the sub-Antarctic Ocean fully lived up to its evil winter reputation. I decided to run north for at least two days while the wind held, and thus get into warmer weather before turning to the east and laying a course for South Georgia.

We took two-hourly spells at the tiller. The men who were not on watch crawled into the sodden sleeping bags and tried to forget their troubles for a period. But there was no comfort in the boat, indeed the first night aboard the boat was one of acute discomfort for us all, and we were heartily glad when dawn came and we could begin to prepare a hot breakfast.

Cramped in our narrow quarters and continually wet from the spray, we suffered severely from cold throughout the journey. We fought the seas and the winds, and at the same time had a daily struggle to keep ourselves alive. At times we were in dire peril. Generally we were encouraged by the knowledge that we were progressing towards the desired land, but there were days and nights when we lay hove to, drifting across the storm-whitened seas, and watching the uprearing masses of water, flung to and fro by Nature in the pride of her strength.

Nearly always there were gales. So small was our boat and so great were the seas that often our sail flapped idly in the calm between the crests of two waves. Then we would climb the next slope, and catch the full fury of the gale where the wool-like whiteness of the breaking water surged around us. But we had our moments of laughter—rare, it is true, but hearty enough.

On the third day out the wind came up strong and worked into a gale from the northwest. We stood away to the east, but the increasing seas discovered the weaknesses of our decking. The continuous blows shifted the box lids and sledge-runners so that the canvas sagged down and accumulated water. Then icy trickles, distinct from the driving sprays, poured fore and aft into the boat. We did what we could to secure the decking, but our means were very limited, and the water continued to enter the boat at a dozen points.

Much bailing was necessary, but nothing could prevent our gear from becoming sodden. The searching runnels from the canvas were really more unpleasant than the sudden definite douches of the sprays. There were no dry places in the boat, and at last we simply covered our heads with our Burberrys and endured the all-pervading water. The bailing was work for the watch.

None of us, however, had any real rest. The perpetual motion of the boat made repose impossible; we were cold, sore and anxious. In the semi-darkness of the day we moved on hands and knees under the decking. By 6 P.M. the darkness was complete, and not until 7 A.M. could we see one another under the thwarts. We had a few scraps of candle, but we preserved them carefully so that we might have light at mealtimes. There was one fairly dry spot in the boat, under the solid original decking at the bows, and there we managed to protect some of our biscuit from the salt water. But I do not think any of us got the taste of salt out of our mouths during the voyage.

The difficulty of movement in the boat would have had its humorous side if it had not caused so many aches and pains. In order to move along the boat we had to crawl under the thwarts, and our knees suffered considerably. When a watch turned out I had to direct each man by name when and where to move, for if all hands had crawled about at the same time the result would have been dire confusion and many bruises.

Then there was the trim of the boat to be considered. The order of the watch was four hours on and four hours off, three men to the watch. One man had the tiller ropes, the second man attended to the sail, and the third bailed for all he was worth. Sometimes, when the water in the boat had been reduced to reasonable proportions, we could use our pump, which Hurley had made from the Flinders' bar case of our ship's standard compass. Though its capacity was small this pump was quite effective. While the new watch was shivering in the wind and spray, the men who had been relieved groped hurriedly among the soaking sleeping bags, and tried to steal some of the warmth created by the last occupants; but it was not always possible to find even this comfort when we went off watch. The boulders which we had taken aboard for ballast had to be shifted continually in order to trim the boat and give access to the pump, which became choked with hairs from the moulting sleeping bags and finneskoe.

The moving of the boulders was weary and painful work. As ballast they were useful, but as weights to be moved about in cramped quarters they were simply appalling. They spared no portion of our poor bodies. Another of our troubles was the chafing of our legs by our wet clothes, and our pain was increased by the bite of the salt water. At the time we thought that we never slept, but in fact we dozed off uncomfortably, to be roused quickly by some new ache or by another call to effort. My own share of the general discomfort was increased by a finely-developed bout of sciatica, which

WHALING SHIPS CAUGHT IN ARCTIC OCEAN ICE

had begun on the floe several months earlier.

Our meals were regular in spite of the gales. Attention to this was essential, since the conditions of the voyage made ever-increasing calls upon our vitality. The meals, which consisted chiefly of Bovril sledging-ration, were the bright beacons in these cold and stormy days. Finding ourselves in need of an oil lamp to eke out our supply of candles, we emptied one of our two tins of Virol in the manner which most appealed to us, and fitted it with a wick made by shredding a bit of canvas. This lamp was of great assistance to us at night. Since we had 6½ gallons of petroleum we were fairly well off for fuel.

A severe southwesterly gale on the fourth day out forced us to heave to. The delay was vexatious, since up to that time we had been making sixty to seventy miles a day, good going with our limited sail area. We hove to under double-reefed mainsail and our little jigger, and waited for the gale to blow itself out. The weather, however, did not improve, and on the fifth day we were obliged to take in the double-reefed mainsail and hoist our small jib instead.

We put out a sea anchor to keep the boat's head up to the sea. This anchor consisted of a triangular canvas bag fastened to the end of the painter and allowed to stream out from the bows. The boat was high enough to catch the wind, and, as she drifted to leeward, the drag of the anchor kept her head to windward. Thus our boat took most of the seas more or less end on, but even then we shipped a great deal of water, which necessitated unceasing bailing and pumping. A thousand times it seemed as if the *James Caird* must be engulfed; but the boat lived.

The gale had its birthplace above the Antarctic continent, and its freezing breath lowered the temperature far towards zero. The spray froze upon the boat and gave bows, sides and decking a heavy coat of mail. This ice reduced the buoyancy of the boat, and to that extent was an added peril; but from one point of view it possessed a notable advantage. The water ceased to drop and trickle from the canvas, and the spray came in solely at the well in the after part of the boat. We could not allow the load of ice to increase beyond a certain point, and in turn we crawled about the decking forward, chipping and picking at it with what tools we had.

When daylight came on the sixth day we saw and felt that the *James Caird* had lost her resiliency. She was not rising to the oncoming seas. The weight of the ice was having its effect, and she was becoming more like a log than a boat. The situation called for immediate action. First of all we broke away the spare oars, which were encased in ice and frozen to the sides of the boat, and threw them overboard. We kept two oars for use when we got inshore. Then two of the fur sleeping bags went over the side, weighing probably forty pounds each. We still had four bags, three in use and one in reserve should a member of the party permanently break down. The reduction of weight relieved the boat to some extent, and vigorous chipping and scraping, by which we got rid of a lot of ice, helped more. The *James Caird* lifted to the endless waves as though she lived again.

About 11 A.M. the boat suddenly fell off into the trough of the sea. The painter had parted and the sea-anchor had gone. This was serious. The boat went away to leeward, and we had no chance to recover the anchor and our valuable rope, which had been our only means of keeping the boat's head up to the sea without the risk of hoisting sail in a gale. Now we had to set the sail and trust to its holding. While the *James Caird* rolled in the trough, we beat the frozen canvas until the bulk of the ice had cracked off it, and then we hoisted it. The frozen gear worked protestingly, but after a struggle our little craft came up to the wind again, and we breathed more freely.

Skin frostbites were troubling us, and we had developed large blisters on our fingers and hands, but we held the boat up to the gale during the day, enduring as best we could discomforts amounting to pain. Our thoughts did not embrace much more than the necessities of the hour. Every surge of the sea was an enemy to be watched and circumvented. Night fell early, and in the lagging hours of darkness we were cheered by an improvement in the weather. The wind dropped, the snow-squalls became less frequent, and the sea moderated.

When the morning of the seventh day dawned there was not much wind, and we shook the reef out of the sail and laid our course once more for South Georgia. The sun came out bright and clear, and presently Worsley got a snap for longitude. We hoped that the sky would remain clear until noon so that we could get the latitude, for we had been six days out without an observation, and our dead reckoning naturally was uncertain.

The boat on that morning must have presented a strange appearance. All hands basked in the sunshine. We hung our sleeping bags to the mast, and our socks and other gear were spread all over the deck. Porpoises came blowing round the boat, and Cape pigeons wheeled and swooped within a few feet of us. These little black-and-white birds have an air of friendliness which is not possessed by the great circling albatross.

We revelled in the warmth of the sun during that day. Life, after all, was not so bad. Our gear was drying, and we could have a hot meal in more or less comfort. The swell was still heavy, but it was not breaking, and the boat rode easily. At noon Worsley balanced himself on the gunwale and clung with one hand to the stay of the mainmast while he got a snap of the sun. The result was more than encouraging. We had done over 380 miles and were getting on for halfway to South Georgia. It looked as if we were going to get through.

During the afternoon the wind freshened to a good stiff breeze, and the *James Caird* made satisfactory progress. I had not realized until the sunlight came how small our boat really was. So low in the water were we that each succeeding swell cut off our view of the sky-line. At one moment the consciousness of the forces arrayed against us would be almost overwhelming, and then hope and confidence would rise again as our boat rose to a wave and tossed aside the crest in a sparkling shower. My gun and some cartridges were stowed aboard the boat as a precaution against a shortage of food, but we were not disposed to destroy our little neighbors, the Cape pigeons, even for the sake of fresh meat. We might have shot an albatross, but the wandering king of the ocean aroused in us something of the feeling that inspired, too late, the Ancient Mariner.

The eighth, ninth and tenth days of the voyage had few features worthy of special note. The wind blew hard during these days, and the strain of navigating the boat was unceasing, but we kept on advancing towards our goal and felt that we were going to succeed. We still suffered severely from the cold, for our vitality was declining owing to shortage of food, exposure, and the necessity of maintaining our cramped positions day and night. I found that it was now absolutely necessary to prepare hot milk for all hands during the night, in order to sustain life until dawn. This involved an increased drain upon our small supply of matches, and our supply already was very small indeed. One of the memories which comes to me of those days is of Crean singing at the tiller. He always sang while he was steering, but nobody ever discovered what the song was.

On the tenth night Worsley could not straighten his body after his spell at the tiller. He was thoroughly cramped, and we had to drag him beneath the decking and massage him before he could unbend himself and get into a sleeping bag.

A hard northwesterly gale came up on the eleventh day (May 5th), and in the late afternoon it shifted to the southwest. The sky was overcast and occasional snow-squalls added to the discomfort produced by a tremendous cross-sea—the worst, I thought, which we had encountered. At midnight I was at the tiller, and suddenly noticed a line of clear sky between the south and southwest. I called to the other men that the sky was clearing, and then, a moment later, realized that what I had seen was not a rift in the clouds but the white crest of an enormous wave.

During twenty-six years' experience of the ocean in all its moods I had never seen a wave so gigantic. It was a mighty upheaval of the ocean, a thing quite apart from the big white-capped seas which had been our tireless enemies for many days. I shouted, "For God's sake, hold on! It's got us!" Then came a moment of suspense which seemed to last for hours. We felt our boat lifted and flung forward like a cork in breaking surf. We were in a seething chaos of tortured water; but somehow the boat lived through it, half full of water, sagging to the dead weight and shuddering under the blow. We bailed with the energy of men fighting for life, flinging the water over the sides with every receptacle which came into our hands; and after ten minutes of uncertainty we felt the boat renew her life beneath us. She floated again, and ceased to lurch drunkenly as though dazed by the attack of the sea. Earnestly we hoped that never again should we encounter such a wave.

The conditions of the boat, uncomfortable before, were made worse by this deluge of water. All our gear was thoroughly wet again, and our cooking-stove was floating about in the bottom of the boat. Not until 3 A.M., when we were all chilled to the limit of endurance, did we manage to get the stove alight and to make ourselves hot drinks. The carpenter was suffering particularly, but he showed grit and spirit. Vincent, however, had collapsed, and for the past week had ceased to be an active member of the crew.

On the following day (May 6th) the weather improved, and we got a glimpse of the sun. Worsley's observation showed that we were not more than 100 miles from the northwest corner of South Georgia. Two more days, with a favorable wind, and we should sight the promised land. I hoped that there would be no delay, as our supply of water was running very low. The hot drink at night was essential, but I decided that the daily allowance of water must be cut down to half a pint per man. Our lumps of ice had gone some days before; we were dependent upon the water which we had brought from Elephant Island, and our thirst was increased by the fact that we were at this time using the brackish water in the breaker which had been slightly stove in when the boat was being loaded. Some seawater had entered it.

Thirst took possession of us, but I dared not permit the allowance of water to be increased, because an unfavorable wind might have driven us away from the island and have lengthened our voyage by several days. Lack of water is always the most severe privation which men can be condemned to endure and we found that the salt water in our clothing and the salt spray which lashed our faces made our thirst quickly grow to a burning pain. I had to be very firm in refusing to allow any one to anticipate the morrow's allowance, which sometimes I was begged to do.

I had altered the course to the east so as to make sure of striking the island, which would have been impossible to regain if we had run past the northern end. The course was laid on our scrap of chart for a point some thirty miles down the coast. That day and the following day passed for us in a sort of nightmare. Our mouths were dry and our tongues were swollen. The wind was still strong and the heavy sea forced us to navigate carefully. But any thought of our peril from the waves was buried beneath the consciousness of our raging thirst. The bright moments were those when we each received our one mug of hot milk during the long, bitter watches of the night.

Things were bad for us in those days, but the end was approaching. The morning of May 8th broke thick and stormy, with squalls from the northwest. We searched the waters ahead for a sign of land, and, although we searched in vain, we were cheered by a sense that the goal was near. About 10 A.M. we passed a little bit of kelp, a glad signal of the proximity of land. An hour later we saw two shags sitting on a big mass of kelp, and we knew then that we must be within ten or fifteen miles of the shore. These birds are as sure an indication of the proximity of land as a lighthouse is, for they never venture far to sea.

We gazed ahead with increasing eagerness, and at 12:30 P.M., through a rift in the clouds, McCarthy caught a glimpse of the black cliffs of South Georgia, just fourteen days after our departure from Elephant Island. It was a glad moment. Thirst-ridden, chilled, and weak as we were, happiness irradiated us. The job was nearly done.

We stood in towards the shore to look for a landing place, and presently we could see the green tussock-grass on the ledges above the surf-beaten rocks. Ahead

NAVIGATING WITH A SEXTANT

of us, and to the south, blind rollers showed the presence of uncharted reefs along the coast. The rocky coast appeared to descend sheer to the sea. Our need of water and rest was almost desperate, but to have attempted a landing at that time would have been suicidal.

Night was approaching and the weather indications were unfavorable. We could do nothing but haul off until the following morning, so we stood away on the starboard tack until we had made what appeared to be a safe offing. Then we hove to in the high westerly swell. The hours passed slowly as we waited the dawn; our thirst was a torment and we could scarcely touch our food, the cold seemed to strike right through our weakened bodies.

At 5 A.M. the wind shifted to the northwest, and quickly increased to one of the worst hurricanes any of us had ever experienced. A great cross-sea was running and the wind simply shrieked as it converted the whole seascape into a haze of driving spray. Down into the valleys, up to tossing heights, straining until her seams opened, swung our little boat, brave still but laboring heavily. We knew that the wind and set of the sea were driving us ashore, but we could do nothing.

The dawn revealed a storm-torn ocean, and the morning passed without bringing us a sight of the land; but at 1 P.M., through a rift in the flying mists, we got a glimpse of the huge crags of the island and realized that our position had become desperate. We were on a dead lee shore, and we could gauge our approach to the unseen cliffs by the roar of the breakers against the sheer walls of rock. I ordered the double-reefed mainsail to be set in the hope that we might claw off, and this attempt increased the strain upon the boat.

The *James Caird* was bumping heavily, and the water was pouring in everywhere. Our thirst was forgotten in the realization of our imminent danger, as we bailed unceasingly and from time to time adjusted our weights; occasional glimpses showed that the shore was nearer.

I knew that Annewkow Island lay to the south of us, but our small and badly marked chart showed uncertain reefs in the passage between the island and the mainland, and I dared not trust it, though, as a last resort, we could try to lie under the lee of the island.

The afternoon wore away as we edged down the coast, and the approach of evening found us still some distance from Annewkow Island; dimly in the twilight we could see a snow-capped mountain looming above us. The chance of surviving the night seemed small, and I think most of us felt that the end was very near. Just after 6 P.M., as the boat was in the yeasty backwash from the seas flung from this iron-bound coast, just when things looked their worst, they changed for the best: so thin is the line which divides success from failure.

The wind suddenly shifted, and we were free once more to make an offing. Almost as soon as the gale eased, the pin which locked the mast to the thwart fell out. Throughout the hurricane it must have been on the point of doing this, and if it had, nothing could have saved us. The mast would have snapped like a carrot. Our backstays had carried away once before, when iced up, and were not too strongly fastened. We were thankful indeed for the mercy which had held the pin in its place during the hurricane.

We stood off shore again, tired almost to the point of apathy. Our water had long been finished. The last was about a pint of hairy liquid, which we strained through a bit of gauze from the medicine chest. The pangs of thirst attacked us with redoubled intensity, and I felt that at almost any risk we must make a landing on the following day. The night wore on. We were very tired and longed for day. When at last dawn came there was hardly any wind, but a high cross-sea was running. We made slow progress towards the shore.

About 8 A.M. the wind backed to the northwest and threatened another blow. In the meantime we had sighted a big indentation which I thought must be King Haakon Bay, and I decided that we must land there. We set the bows of the boat towards the bay, and ran before the freshening gale. Soon we had angry reefs on either side. Great glaciers came down to the sea and offered no landing place. The sea spouted on the reefs and thundered against the shore. About noon we sighted a line of jagged reef, like blackened teeth, which seemed to bar the entrance to the bay. Inside, fairly smooth water stretched eight or nine miles to the head of the bay.

A gap in the reef appeared, and we made for it, but the fates had another rebuff for us. The wind shifted and blew from the east right out of the bay. We could see the way through the reef, but we could not approach it directly. That afternoon we bore up, tacking five times in the strong wind. The last tack enabled us to get through, and at last we were in the wide mouth of the bay.

Dusk was approaching. A small cove, with a boulder-strewn beach guarded by a reef, made a break in the cliffs on the south side of the bay, and we turned in that direction. I stood in the bows, and directed the steering as we ran through the kelp and made the passage of the reef. The entrance was so narrow that we had to take in the oars, and the swell was piling itself right over the reef into the cove. But in a minute or two we were inside, and in the gathering darkness the *James Caird* ran in on a swell and touched the beach.

I sprang ashore with the short painter, and held on when the boat went out with the backward surge. When the boat came in again three men got ashore and held the painter while I climbed some rocks with another line. A slip on the wet rocks twenty feet up nearly closed my part of the story, just when we were achieving safety. A jagged piece of rock held me and also sorely bruised me. I, however, made fast the line, and in a few minutes we were all safe on the beach, with the boat floating in the surging water just off the shore.

We heard a gurgling sound which was sweet music in our ears, and, peering round, we found a stream of fresh water almost at our feet. A moment later we were down on our knees drinking the pure, ice-cold water in long draughts which put new life into us. It was a splendid moment.

A British explorer, Sir Ernest Henry Shackleton (1874–1922) commanded a south polar expedition in 1907 during which the south magnetic pole was located. In his book South, *he describes an expedition in 1914 when his ship, the* Endurance, *was crushed in the ice. He led his party to safety and then had to sail in a tiny open boat for help. This story is about that incredible sixteen-day passage on the sub-Antarctic Ocean.*

Halfway

Thor Heyerdahl

We were visited by whales many times, most often they were small porpoises and toothed whales which gambolled about us in large schools on the surface of the water, but now and then there were big cachalots, too, and other giant whales which appeared singly or in small schools. Sometimes they passed like ships on the horizon, now and again sending a cascade of water into the air, but sometimes they steered straight for us. We were prepared for a dangerous collision the first time a big whale altered course and came straight toward the raft in a purposeful manner. As it gradually drew nearer, we could hear its blowing and puffing, heavy and long drawn, each time it rolled its head out of the water. It was an enormous, thick-skinned, ungainly land animal that came toiling through the water, as unlike a fish as a bat is unlike a bird. It came straight toward our port side, where we stood gathered on the edge of the raft, while one man sat at the masthead and shouted that he could see seven or eight more making their way toward us.

The big, shining, black forehead of the first whale was not more than two yards from us when it sank beneath the surface of the water, and then we saw the enormous blue-black bulk glide quietly under the raft right beneath our feet. It

lay there for a time, dark and motionless, and we held our breath as we looked down on the gigantic curved back of a mammal a good deal longer than the whole raft. Then it sank slowly through the bluish water and disappeared from sight. Meanwhile the whole school was close upon us, but they paid no attention to us. Whales that have abused their giant strength and sunk whaling boats with their tails have presumably been attacked first. The whole morning we had them puffing and blowing round us in the most unexpected places without their even pushing against the raft or the steering oar. They quite enjoyed themselves gambolling freely among the waves in the sunshine. But about noon the whole school dived as if on a given signal and disappeared for good.

It was not only whales we could see under the raft. If we lifted up the reed matting we slept on, through the chinks between the logs we saw right down into the crystal-blue water. If we lay thus for a while, we saw a breast fin or tail fin waggle past and now and again we saw a whole fish. If the chinks had been a few inches wider, we could have lain comfortably in bed with a line and fished under our mattresses.

The fish which most of all attached themselves to the raft were dolphins and pilot fish.

From the moment the first dolphins joined us in the current off Callao, there was not a day on the whole voyage on which we had not large dolphins wriggling round us. What drew them to the raft we do not know, but, either there was a magical attraction in being able to swim in the shade with a moving roof above them, or there was food to be found in our kitchen garden of seaweed and barnacles that hung like garlands from all the logs and from the steering oar. It began with a thin coating of smooth green, but then the clusters of seaweed grew with astonishing speed, so that the *Kon-Tiki* looked like a bearded sea-god as she tumbled along among the waves. Inside the green seaweed was a favorite resort of tiny small fry and our stowaways, the crabs.

There was a time when ants began to get the upper hand on board. There had been small black ants in some of the logs, and, when we had got to sea and the damp began to penetrate into the wood, the ants swarmed out and into the sleeping bags. They were all over the place, and bit and tormented us till we thought they would drive us off the raft. But gradually, as it became wetter out at sea, they realized that this was not their right element, and only a few isolated specimens held out till we reached the other side. What did best on the raft, along with the crabs, were barnacles from an inch to an inch and a half long. They grew in hundreds, especially on the lee side of the raft, and as fast as we put the old ones into the soup kettle new larvae took root and grew up. The barnacles tasted fresh and delicate; we picked the seaweed as salad and it was eatable, though not so good. We never actually saw the dolphins feeding in the vegetable garden, but they were constantly turning their gleaming bellies upward and swimming under the logs.

The dolphin (dorado), which is a brilliantly colored tropical fish, must not be confused with the creature, also called dolphin, which is a small, toothed whale. The dolphin was ordinarily from three feet three inches to four feet six inches long and had much flattened sides with an enormously high head and neck. We jerked on board one which was four feet eight inches long with a head thirteen and one-half inches high. The dolphin had a magnificent color. In the water it shone blue and green like a bluebottle with a glitter of golden-yellow fins. But if we hauled one on board, we some-

times saw a strange sight. As the fish died, it gradually changed color and became silver gray with black spots and, finally, a quite uniform silvery white. This lasted for four or five minutes, and then the old colors slowly reappeared. Even in the water the dolphin could occasionally change color like a chameleon, and often we saw a "new kind" of shining copper-colored fish, which on a closer acquaintance proved to be our old companion the dolphin.

The high forehead gave the dolphin the appearance of a bulldog flattened from the side, and it always cut through the surface of the water when the predatory fish shot off like a torpedo after a fleeing shoal of flying fish. When the dolphin was in a good humor, it turned over on its flat side, went ahead at a great speed, and then sprang high into the air and tumbled down like a flat pancake. It came down on the surface with a regular smack and a column of water rose up. It was no sooner down in the water than it came up in another leap, and yet another, away over the swell. But, when it was in a bad temper—for example, when we hauled it up on to the raft—then it bit. Torstein limped about for some time with a rag round his big toe because he had let it stray into the mouth of a dolphin, which had used the opportunity to close its jaws and chew a little harder than usual. After our return home we heard that dolphins attack and eat people when bathing. This was not very complimentary to us, seeing that we had bathed among them every day without their showing any particular interest. But they were formidable beasts of prey, for we found both squids and whole flying fish in their stomachs.

Flying fish were the dolphins' favorite food. If anything splashed on the surface of the water, they rushed at it blindly in the hope of its being a flying fish. In many a drowsy morning hour, when we crept blinking out of the cabin and, half asleep, dipped a toothbrush into the sea, we became wide awake with a jump when a thirty-pound fish shot out like lightning from under the raft and nosed at the toothbrush in disappointment. And, when we were sitting quietly at breakfast on the edge of the raft, a dolphin might jump up and make one of its most vigorous sideway splashes, so that the sea water ran down our backs and into our food.

One day, when we were sitting at dinner, Torstein made a reality of the tallest of fish stories. He suddenly

THE PLAYA, PANAMA

laid down his fork and put his hand into the sea, and, before we knew what was happening, the water was boiling and a big dolphin came tumbling in among us. Torstein had caught hold of the tail end of a fishing line which came quietly gliding past, and on the other end hung a completely astonished dolphin which had broken Erik's line when he was fishing a few days before.

There was not a day on which we had not six or seven dolphins following us in circles round and under the raft. On bad days there might be only two or three, but, on the other hand, as many as thirty or forty might turn up the day after. As a rule it was enough to warn the cook twenty minutes in advance if we wanted fresh fish for dinner. Then he tied a line to a short bamboo stick and put half a flying fish on the hook. A dolphin was there in a flash, plowing the surface with its head as it chased the hook, with two or three more in its wake. It was a splendid fish to play and, when freshly caught, its flesh was firm and delicious to eat, like a mixture of cod and salmon. It kept for two days, and that was all we needed, for there were fish enough in the sea.

We became acquainted with pilot fish in another way. Sharks brought them and left them to be adopted by us after the sharks' death. We had not been long at sea before the first shark visited us. And sharks soon became an almost daily occurrence. Sometimes the shark just came swimming up to inspect the raft and went on in search of prey after circling round us once or twice. But most often the sharks took up a position in our wake just behind the steering oar, and there they lay without a sound, stealing from starboard to port and occasionally giving a leisurely wag of their tails to keep pace with the raft's placid advance. The blue-gray body of the shark always looked brownish in the sunlight just below the surface, and it moved up and down with the seas so that the dorsal fin always stuck up menacingly. If there was a high sea, the shark might be lifted up by the waves high above our own level, and we had a direct side view of the shark as in a glass case as it swam toward us in a dignified manner with its fussy retinue of small pilot fish ahead of its jaws. For a few seconds it looked as if both the shark and its striped companions would swim right on board, but then the raft would lean over gracefully to leeward, rise over the ridge of waves, and descend on the other side.

To begin with, we had a great respect for sharks on

32

account of their reputation and their alarming appearance. There was an unbridled strength in the streamlined body, consisting of one great bundle of steel muscles, and a heartless greed in the broad flat head with the small, green cat's eyes and the enormous jaws which could swallow footballs. When the man at the helm shouted "Shark alongside to starboard" or "Shark alongside to port," we used to come out in search of hand harpoons and gaffs and station ourselves along the edge of the raft. The shark usually glided round us with the dorsal fin close up to the logs. And our respect for the shark increased when we saw that the gaffs bent like spaghetti when we struck them against the sandpaper armor on the shark's back, while the spearheads of the hand harpoons were broken in the heat of the battle. All we gained by getting through the shark's skin and into the gristle or muscle was a hectic struggle, in which the water boiled round us till the shark broke loose and was off, while a little oil floated up and spread itself out over the surface.

To save our last harpoon head we fastened together a bunch of our largest fishhooks and hid them inside the carcass of a whole dolphin. We slung the bait overboard with a precautionary multiplication of steel lines fastened to a piece of our own lifeline. Slowly and surely the shark came, and, as it lifted its snout above the water, it opened its great crescent-shaped jaws with a jerk and let the whole dolphin slip in and down. And there it stuck. There was a struggle in which the shark lashed the water into foam, but we had a good grip on the rope and hauled the big fellow, despite its resistance, as far as the logs aft, where it lay awaiting what might come and only gaped as though to intimidate us with its parallel rows of sawlike teeth. Here we profited by a sea to slide the shark up over the low end logs, slippery with seaweed and, after casting a rope round the tail fin, we ran well out of the way till the war dance was over.

In the gristle of the first shark we caught this way we found our own harpoon head, and we thought at first that this was the reason for the shark's comparatively small fighting spirit. But later we caught shark after shark by the same method, and every time it went just as easily. Even if the shark could jerk and tug and certainly was fearfully heavy to play, it became quite spiritless and tame and never made full use of its giant strength if we only managed to hold the line tight without letting the shark gain an inch in the tug of war. The sharks we got on board were usually from six to ten feet long, and there were blue sharks as well as brown sharks. The last-named had a skin outside the mass of muscles through which we could not drive a sharp knife unless we struck with our whole strength, and often not even then. The skin of the belly was as impenetrable as that of the back; the five gill clefts behind the head on each side were the only vulnerable point.

When we hauled in a shark, black slippery remora fish were usually fixed tight to its body. By means of an oval sucking disc on the top of the flat head, they were fastened so tight that we could not get them loose by pulling their tails. But they themselves could break loose and skip away to take hold at another place in a second. If they grew tired of hanging tightly to the shark when their host gave no sign of returning to the sea, they leaped off and vanished down between the chinks in the raft to swim away and find themselves another shark. If the remora does not find a shark, it attaches itself to the skin of another fish for the time being. It is generally as long as the length of a finger up to a foot. We tried the natives' old trick which they sometimes use when they have been lucky enough to secure a live remora. They tie a line to its tail and let it swim away. It then tries to suck itself on to the first fish it sees and clings so tightly that a lucky fisherman may haul in both fishes by the remora's tail. We had no luck. Every single time we let a remora go with a line tied to its tail, it simply shot off and sucked itself fast to one of the logs of the raft, in the belief that it had found an extra fine, big shark. And there it hung, however hard we tugged on the line. We gradually acquired a number of these small remoras which hung on and dangled obstinately among the shells on the side of the raft, travelling with us right across the Pacific.

But the remora was stupid and ugly and never became such an agreeable pet as its lively companion the pilot fish. The pilot fish is a small cigar-shaped fish with zebra stripes, which swims rapidly in a shoal ahead of the shark's snout. It received its name because it was thought that it piloted its half-blind friend the shark about in the sea. In reality, it simply goes along with the shark, and, if it acts independently, it is only because it catches sight of food within its own range of vision. The pilot fish accompanied its lord and master to the last second. But, as it could not cling fast to the giant's skin, as the remora does, it was completely bewildered when its old master suddenly disappeared up into the air and did not come down again. Then the pilot fish scurried about in a distracted manner, searching wildly, but always came back and wriggled along astern of the raft, where the shark had vanished skyward. But as time passed and the shark did not come down again, they had to look round for a new lord and master. And none was nearer to hand than the *Kon-Tiki* herself.

If we let ourselves down over the side of the raft, with our heads down in the brilliantly clear water, we saw the raft as the belly of a sea monster, with the steering oar as its tail and the centerboards hanging down like blunt fins. In between them all the adopted pilot fish swam, side by side, and took no notice of the bubbling human head except that one or two of them darted swiftly aside and peered right up its nose, only to wriggle back again unperturbed and take their places in the ranks of eager swimmers. Our pilot fish patrolled in two detachments: most of them swam between the centerboards, the others in a graceful fan formation ahead of the bow. Now and then they shot away from the raft to snap up some edible trifle we passed, and after meals, when we washed our crockery in the water alongside, it was as if we had emptied a whole cigar case of striped pilot fish among the scraps. There was not a single scrap they did not examine, and, so long as it was not vegetable food, down it went. These queer little fish huddled under our protecting wings with such childlike confidence that we, like the shark, had a fatherly protective feeling toward them. They became the *Kon-Tiki*'s marine pets, and it was taboo on board to lay hands on a pilot fish.

We had in our retinue pilot fish which were certainly in their childhood for they were hardly an inch long, while most were about six inches. When the whale shark rushed off at lightning speed after Erik's harpoon had entered its skull, some of its old pilot fish strayed over to the victor; they were two feet long. After a succession of victories the *Kon-Tiki* soon had a following of forty or fifty pilot fish, and many of them liked our quiet forward movement, and our daily scraps, so much that they followed us for thousands of miles over the sea.

But occasionally some were faithless. One day, when I was at the steering oar, I suddenly noticed that the sea was boiling to southward and saw an immense shoal of dolphins come shooting across the sea like silver torpedoes. They did not come as usual, splashing along comfortably on their flat sides, but came rushing at frantic speed more through the air than through the water. The blue swell was whipped into white foam in one single turmoil of splashing fugitives, and behind them came a black back dashing along on a zigzag course like a speedboat. The desperate dolphins came shooting through and over the surface right up to the raft; here they dived, while about a hundred crowded together in a tightly packed shoal and swung away to eastward, so that the whole sea astern was a glittering mass of colors. The gleaming back behind them half rose above the surface, dived in a graceful curve under the raft, and shot astern after the shoal of dolphins. It was a devilish-big fellow of a blue shark that seemed to be nearly twenty feet long. When it disappeared, a number of our pilot fish had gone too. They had found a more exciting sea hero to go campaigning with.

A Norwegian explorer who sought evidence that ancient cultures could have crossed the oceans, Thor Heyerdahl (b. 1914) sailed across the Pacific, the Atlantic, and the Persian Gulf in replicas of primitive crafts. He describes these voyages in Kon Tiki *(1948). This selection is about his trip from South America to the South Pacific in a pre-Columbian raft.*

ABOVE: LOW TIDE, LOWER ST. LAWRENCE RIVER, QUEBEC
BELOW: CORNWALL, ENGLAND

The Attack of the Spanish Armada

Hilaire Belloc

The Straits of Dover, when one approaches them from the east, are like the mouth of a great river, nor do they ever bear that aspect more than at sunset, when, if one is in mid-stream and the day has been clear, one sees quite close upon either hand, not ten miles off each way, the highlands of either shore, those highlands branching outwards till they are lost on the horizon as might be lost the spreading highlands of an estuary.

If the stream be at the ebb the illusion is enhanced, for one sees the pouring out of the flood in the way that a river should go; it is then not difficult to forget the North Sea behind one, and to imagine, as one drifts down the mid-channel towards the color in the west, that one is still embraced by the land and that one is only just now setting out to sea. The sun broadens into a long belt of haze before it touches the horizon, and the light of it catches either line of cliffs. It seems a very peaceful sea.

July 27, 1588, was of this kind. The sun was setting beyond the shoals of the Varne and all the great roundell of Spanish ships were clustered in a group from Gris-Nez eastward, coming up very slowly against the tide; they sailed above an easy holding-ground not far from the French land. The huge bulk of the transports, high forward and astern, cast long shadows upon the calm; it was the merest breath of wind that carried the Armada on, or rather, just held it against the strong coastwise stream. When the last of them and the slowest had passed outside the shoals that cluster under the steep of Gris-Nez the rattling of chains began through the clear and silent air; there were signals both with bugle and with bunting, a gun was fired, and the wide fleet dropped anchor in fifteen fathom and rode, every ship with its bows upstream and every high poop in the blaze of the sunset. It was Saturday evening. All week long they had crawled and beaten up the Channel, and all week long the little English craft with their much heavier artillery had stood the recoil of their own great guns and had peppered the enemy from well out of range; and one ship the Spaniards had lost by collision so that she lagged and Drake caught her, full of gold, and another a traitor had fired, and this also, or the charred hulk of it, had been towed into an English harbor.

The Lord Admiral of England all that week had followed in the *Ark-Royall*. He had followed them by day and by night; all the hours a man can see to fire he ordered the intermittent cannonade, and now upon this calm evening, with the northerly breeze gone westward and dying down, he and his came up between the Spaniards and the sun. They also cast anchor just out of range, and from beyond the Straits from round the North Foreland came thirty more from London and joined the line.

It was soon dark. Long before midnight the craft began to swing, the smaller English vessels coming quickly round to the bubbling of the flood tide as it swirled round Gris-Nez, the larger Spanish transports catching the stream more slowly, but at last turned also east and west to the change of the sea, and with the turn of the tide the wind rose, though at first but little, and blew steadily out of the west and south in a gentle and constant manner, and the sky clouded. The beacon upon Dover cliff flickered far off to the west and the northward; one could see bonfires or the glare of them against the sky of the Weald, and there were more lights than usual passing up and down the English shore. Upon the French, the tall Pharos of Calais alone shone over the marshy flats. Gris-Nez was a huge lump against the darkness. But all the surface of the sea was dotted with the lamps of the fleets and the broken water was full of glints and reflections.

In Dunkirk, a very few miles up the shore, waited that army which, if in any manner it could have crossed the day's march of salt water, would have raised the Catholic north of England, occupied the indifferent south, and held London—to the complete reversal of the fate of Europe. Further still up coast, at Nieuport, was their reserve. It was midnight and past midnight; the Sunday morning had begun, and the wind, chopping a little northward and uncertain, but in general a little south of west, blew in gusts that soon joined to half a gale. The sea rose, and along the line of the sand and under the dark steep beyond, the long white line of breakers was very clear through the darkness.

Aboard the *Ark-Royall* the Lord Admiral Howard, the landsman, took counsel and did as he was told. They took eight ships of the worst, cleared them and stuffed them with all manner of burnable and missile things, they put in barrels of pitch and of powder, great stones and round shot, beams of dry wood and slack cordage. They warped them round in the difficulty and tossing of that weather till they pointed up stream, and they set square sails on each that the wind should catch them, so that with the gale and the flood tide together they might bear down upon the Spanish Fleet. These derelicts were held by warps from the stern, and the sails so set strained the warps too powerfully until the signal was given. Then, with great dispatch, the last men left aboard touched fire to matches in twenty places upon one or the other, and tumbled over the side. The strands that held them were cut, and as the first flames leapt from their decks they careered before the wind against the Armada. It was about two o'clock in the morning.

From the *Ark-Royall*, at the head of the English line, was a sight not seen again in history. The conflagration burnt up enormous, clear and high, blazing first from the sterns of the fireships and showing the square sails brilliant red against the night. The gale blew the flames before it in broad sheets, and one could hear the roaring of them even against the wind. Down weather that floating town of Spanish galleys shone out as the dreadful light came near; the tumbling and foaming sea in a circle all around was conspicuous in the strong glare, and the shape of every wave was marked clearly for a cable's length around.

The Armada awoke. Among the thousands who crowded the decks, impeding the haste of the sailors as they ran to let the anchors go, were many who remembered that same awful sight upon the Scheldt three years before, when the fireships had driven against Parma's boom. There was no time for the slow work of the capstans; men took axes and hacked at the cables forward; the canvas was run up as might be in such a medley, and the monstrous bulks paid round in very varied manner, confused and hampering one another as their headsails, with the sheets hard aweather, caught the gale. Not a few, on whom too much had been set or too hastily, careened a moment dangerously to leeward, then recovered; there were shouts everywhere and a babel of orders; men running with fenders to hang over the sides, as one big wall of wood or another surged up too near in the darkness; at last all were turned and free, and the herd of them went driving before the southwest wind along that perilous shore. The men on the *Ark-Royall* and the Lord Admiral, watching from the height of the rail, cursed to see no fireship get home. The set of the seas and the slant of the wind drove one after another upon the flat stretches of the beach, and there they burnt out, bumping higher and higher as the tide rose along the flats, and to their burning was added dull explosions as the fire reached their powder. But the Spanish Fleet was gone.

The *Ark-Royall* also weighed anchor and all her sisters with her to take up that long chase again. It seemed that the attempt had failed—but with the weather that was to be and the port of embarkation passed, the invasion could never come; this island had been certainly saved before the stormy morning broke beyond the marshes of the lowlands.

There was lightning all over heaven before it was day, and the raging water was a little tamed by cataracts of rain. The light grew dully through the furious weather, the Spanish line was scattered twenty miles thwart of the Flanders shore; their leading ships could see the opening of Ostend, their laggards were still far west of Nieuport and near their panic of the night. Off Gravelines the long-range artillery of the English caught them. In spite of the gale each fleet rallied to the sound of the cannon, and all that Sunday long the guns answered each other without a pause, but the English had the range and the weather, and the gigantic Spanish fabrics, leaning away from the blast, shot short or high, while the English broadsides, leaning downward and toward the mark, poured in an accurate fire; those smaller vessels also turned well and quickly even in such a sea, making of themselves a changing target, but having fixed targets before them in the lumbering masses of their opponents. The success of their gunnery lent them hardihood, and the more daring would sweep quite close to the Spanish sides and sheer off again; so was Drake's ship chiefly struck. Had he chosen he might have avoided any such offense and have done his work at full range and in safety, but he was warm to it, and the dancing maneuver pleased him. He was hulled forty times, but he swam.

When the night fell this running business had got off the mouth of the Scheldt. The wind backed a little and blew stronger, but no longer toward the land; the great Armada ran northward before it into the midst of a widening sea, and so up and away, and an end to the great concern.

Born in France but a British subject by 1902, Hilaire Belloc (1870–1953) was a politician and an excellent yachtsman. This account of the British defeating the Spanish Armada, from The Eyewitness *was taken from eyewitness reports. In 1588 Philip II of Spain sent his Armada to invade England. The English sent fire ships into the ranks of the Armada to scatter them and then to attack the fleeing ships at close range. The "undefeatable" Armada lost about half its ships.*

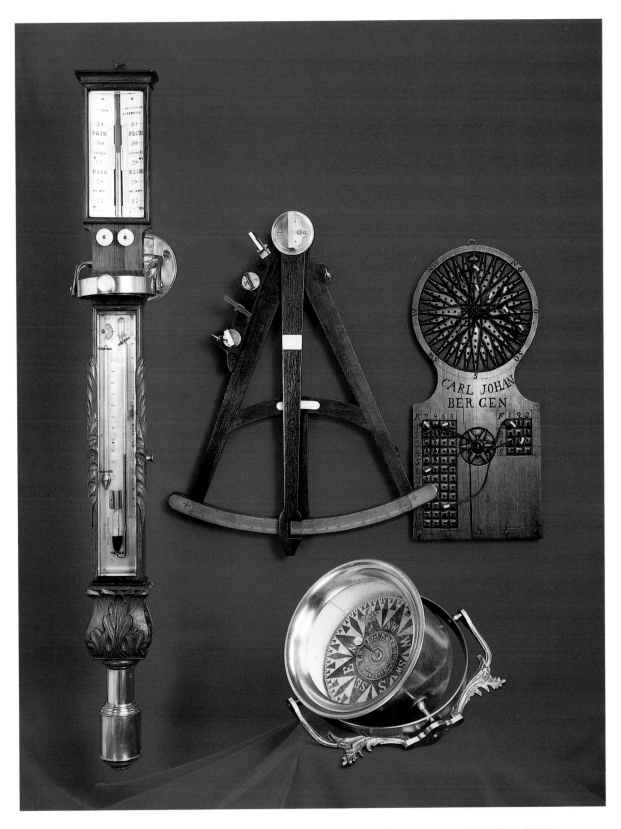

NAVIGATIONAL INSTRUMENTS USED ON NINETEENTH CENTURY SAILING SHIPS

Shipwreck of the Whaleship Essex

Owen Chase

I

The town of Nantucket, in the state of Massachusetts, contains about eight thousand inhabitants; nearly a third part of the population are Quakers, and they are, taken together, a very industrious and enterprising people. On this island are owned about one hundred vessels, of all descriptions, engaged in the whale trade, giving constant employment and support to upwards of sixteen hundred hardy seamen, a class of people proverbial for their intrepidity. This fishery is not carried on to any extent from any other part of the United States, except from the town of New Bedford, directly opposite to Nantucket, where are owned probably twenty sail.

A voyage generally lasts about two years and a half, and with an entire uncertainty of success. Sometimes they are repaid with speedy voyages and profitable cargoes, and at others they drag out a listless and disheartening cruise, without scarcely making the expenses of an outfit. The business is considered a very hazardous one, arising from unavoidable accidents in carrying on an exterminating warfare against those great leviathans of the deep; and indeed a Nantucket man is on all occasions fully sensi-

ble of the honor and merit of his profession; no doubt because he knows that his laurels, like the soldier's, are plucked form the brink of danger. Numerous anecdotes are related of the whalemen of Nantucket; and stories of hair-breadth 'scapes, and sudden and wonderful preservation, are handed down amongst them, with the fidelity, and no doubt many of them with the characteristic fictions, of the ancient legendary tales. A spirit of adventure amongst the sons of other relatives of those immediately concerned in it takes possession of their minds at a very early age. Captivated with the tough stories of the elder seamen, and seduced, as well by the natural desire of seeing foreign countries, as by the hopes of gain, they launch forth six or eight thousand miles from home, into an almost untraversed ocean, and spend from two to three years of their lives in scenes of constant peril, labor, and watchfulness. The profession is one of great ambition, and full of honorable excitement: a tame man is never known amongst them; and the coward is marked with that peculiar aversion that distinguishes our public naval service. There are perhaps no people of superior corporeal powers; and it has been truly said of them that they possess a natural aptitude, which seems rather the lineal spirit of their fathers than the effects of any experience.

The town itself, during the war, was (naturally to have been expected), on the decline; but with the return of peace it took a fresh start, and a spirit for carrying on the fishery received a renewed and very considerable excitement. Large capitals are now embarked; and some of the finest ships our countries can boast of are employed in it. The increased demand, within a few years past, from the spermaceti manufactories, has induced companies and individuals in different parts of the Union to become engaged in the business; and if the future consumption of the manufactured article bears any proportion to that of the past few years, this species of commerce will bid fair to become the most profitable and extensive that our country possesses. From the accounts of those who were in the early stages of the fishery concerned in it, it would appear that the whales had been driven, like the beasts of the forest, before the march of civilization, into remote and more unfrequented seas, until now, they are followed by the enterprise and perseverance of our seamen, even to the distant coasts of Japan.

The ship *Essex*, commanded by Captain George Pollard, junior, was fitted out at Nantucket and sailed on the 12th day of August, 1819, for the Pacific Ocean, on a whaling voyage. Of this ship I was first mate. She had lately undergone a thorough repair in her upper works, and was at that time, in all respects, a sound, substantial vessel. She had a crew of twenty-one men, and was victualled and provided for two years and a half. We left the coast of America with a fine breeze, and steered for the Western Islands.

On the second day out, while sailing moderately on our course in the Gulf Stream, a sudden squall of wind struck the ship from the SW and knocked her completely on her beam-ends, stove one of our boats, entirely destroyed two others, and threw down the cambouse. We distinctly saw the approach of this gust, but miscalculated altogether as to the strength and violence of it. It struck the ship about three points off the weather quarter, at the moment that the man at the helm was in the act of putting her away to run before it. In an instant she was knocked down with her yards in the water; and before hardly a moment of time was allowed for reflection, she gradually came to the wind and righted.

The squall was accompanied with vivid flashes of lightning, and heavy and repeated claps of thunder. The whole ship's crew were, for a short time, thrown into the utmost consternation and confusion; but fortunately the violence of the squall was all contained in the first gust of the wind, and it soon gradually abated, and became fine weather again. We repaired our damage with little difficulty, and continued on our course with the loss of the two boats.

On the 30th of August we made the island of Flores, one of the Western group called the Azores. We lay off and on the island for two days, during which time our boats landed and obtained a supply of vegetables and a few hogs. From this place we took the NE tradewind, and in sixteen days made the Isle of May, one of the Cape Verdes. As we were sailing along the shore of this island, we discovered a ship stranded on the beach, and from her appearance took her to be a whaler. Having lost two of our boats, and presuming that this vessel had probably some belonging to her that might have been saved, we determined to ascertain the name of the ship, and endeavor to supply if possible the loss of our boats from her. We accordingly stood in towards the port, or landing place. After a short time three men were discovered coming out to us in a whale boat. In a few moments they were alongside, and informed us that the wreck was the *Archimedes* of New York, Captain George B. Coffin, which vessel had struck on a rock near the island about a fortnight previously; that all hands were saved by running the ship on shore, and that the captain and the crew had gone home. We purchased the whaleboat of these people, obtained some few more pigs, and again set sail.

Our passage thence to Cape Horn was not distinguished for any incident worthy of note. We made the longitude of the Cape about the 18th of December, having experienced head winds for nearly the whole distance. We anticipated a moderate time in passing this noted land, from the season of the year at which we were there, being considered the most favorable; but instead of this, we experienced heavy westerly gales, and a most tremendous sea, that detained us off the Cape five weeks, before we had got sufficiently to the westward to enable us to put away. Of the passage of this famous Cape it may be observed, that strong westerly gales and a heavy sea are its almost universal atten-

THE SPERMACETI WHALE
Beale.   South Seas.

A WHALEBOAT IN POSITION FOR HARPOONING A SPERM WHALE

dants: the prevalence and constancy of this wind and sea necessarily produce a rapid current, by which vessels are sent to leeward; and it is not without some favorable slant of wind that they can in many cases get round at all. The difficulties and dangers of the passage are proverbial; but as far as my own observation extends (and which the numerous reports of the whalemen corroborate), you can always rely upon a long and regular sea; and although the gales may be very strong and stubborn, as they undoubtedly are, they are not known to blow with the destructive violence that characterizes some of the tornadoes of the western Atlantic Ocean.

On the 17th of January, 1820, we arrived at the island of St. Mary's, lying on the coast of Chile, in latitude 36° 59' south, longitude 73° 41' west. This island is a sort of rendezvous for whalers, from which they obtain their wood and water, and between which and the main land (a distance of about ten miles) they frequently cruise for a species of whale called the right whale. Our

object in going in there was mainly to get the news. We sailed thence to the island of Massafuera, where we got some wood and fish, and thence for the cruising ground along the coast of Chile, in search of the spermaceti whale. We took there eight, which yielded us two hundred and fifty barrels of oil; and the season having by this time expired, we changed our cruising ground to the coast of Peru. We obtained there five hundred and fifty barrels. After going into the small port of Decamas, and replenishing our wood and water, on the 2nd October we set sail for the Galápagos Islands. We came to anchor, and laid seven days off Hood's Island, one of the group; during which time we stopped a leak which we had discovered, and obtained three hundred turtle. We then visited Charles Island, where we procured sixty more. These turtle are a most delicious food, and average in weight generally about one hundred pounds, but many of them weigh upwards of eight hundred. With these, ships usually supply themselves for a great

42

Stewart del.   Lauts sc.

THE SPERMACETI WHALE South Seas.
Beale

THE SPERM WHALE SUCCUMBS, BUT SWAMPS THE WHALEBOAT

length of time, and make a great saving of other provisions. They neither eat nor drink, nor is the least pains taken with them; they are strewed over the deck, thrown under foot, or packed away in the hold, as it suits convenience. They will live upwards of a year without food or water, but soon die in a cold climate.

We left Charles Island on the 23rd of October, and steered off to the westward, in search of whales. In latitude 1° 0' south, longitude 118° west. On the 16th of November, in the afternoon, we lost a boat during our work in a shoal of whales. I was in the boat myself, with five others, and was standing in the forepart, with the harpoon in my hand, well braced, expecting every instant to catch sight of one of the shoal which we were in, that I might strike; but judge of my astonishment and dismay, at finding myself suddenly thrown up in the air, my companions scattered about me, and the boat fast filling with water. A whale had come up directly under her, and with one dash of his tail, had stove

her bottom in, and strewed us in every direction around her. We, however, with little difficulty, got safely on the wreck, and clung there until one of the other boats which had been engaged in the shoal, came to our assistance, and took us off. Strange to tell, not a man was injured by this accident. Thus it happens very frequently in the whaling business, that boats are stove; oars, harpoons, and lines broken; ankles and wrists sprained; boats upset, and whole crews left for hours in the water, without any of these accidents extending to the loss of life. We are so much accustomed to the continual recurrence of such scenes as these, that we become familiarized to them, and consequently always feel that confidence and self-possession, which teaches us every expedient in danger, and inures the body, as well as the mind, to fatigue, privation, and peril, in frequent cases exceeding belief. It is this danger and hardship that makes the sailor; indeed it is the distinguishing qualification amongst us; and it is a common boast of the whaleman, that he has escaped from sudden and apparently inevitable destruction oftener than his fellow. He is accordingly valued on this account, without much reference to other qualities.

II

I have not been able to recur to the scenes which are now to become the subject of description, although a considerable time has elapsed, without feeling a mingled emotion of horror and astonishment at the almost incredible destiny that has preserved me and my surviving companions from a terrible death. Frequently, in my reflections on the subject, even after this lapse of time, I find myself shedding tears of gratitude for our deliverance, and blessing God, by whose divine aid and protection we were conducted through a series of unparalleled suffering and distress, and restored to the bosom of our families and friends. There is no knowing what a stretch of pain and misery the human mind is capable of contemplating, when it is wrought upon by the anxieties of preservation; nor what pangs and weaknesses the body is able to endure, until they are visited upon it; and when at last deliverance comes, when the dream of hope is realized, unspeakable gratitude takes possession of the soul, and tears of joy choke the utterance. We require to be taught in the school of some signal suffering, privation, and despair, the great lessons of constant dependence upon an almighty forbearance and mercy. In the midst of the wide ocean, at night, when the sight of the heavens was shut out, and the dark tempest came upon us; then it was, that we felt ourselves ready to exclaim, "Heaven have mercy upon us, for naught but that can save us now." But I proceed to the recital.

On the 20th of November (cruising in latitude 0° 40' south, longitude 119° 0' west), a shoal of whales was discovered off the lee bow. The weather at this time was extremely fine and clear, and it was about 8 o'clock in the morning, that the man at the masthead gave the usual cry of "there she blows." The ship was immediately put away, and we ran down in the direction for them. When we had got within half a mile of the place where they were observed, all our boats were lowered down, manned, and we started in pursuit of them.

The ship, in the mean time, was brought to the wind, and the main-topsail hove aback, to wait for us. I

had the harpoon in the second boat; the captain preceded me in the first. When I arrived at the spot where we calculated they were, nothing was at first to be seen. We lay on our oars in anxious expectation of discovering them come up somewhere near us. Presently one rose, and spouted a short distance ahead of my boat; I made all speed towards it, came up with, and struck it. Feeling the harpoon in him, he threw himself, in an agony, over towards the boat (which at the time was up alongside of him), and giving a severe blow with his tail, struck the boat near the edge of the water, amidships, and stove a hole in her. I immediately took up the boat hatchet, and cut the line, to disengage the boat from the whale, which by this time was running off with great velocity. I succeeded in getting clear of him, with the loss of the harpoon and line and finding the water to pour fast in the boat, I hastily stuffed three or four of our jackets in the hole, ordered one man to keep constantly bailing, and the rest to pull immediately for the ship. We succeeded in keeping the boat free, and shortly gained the ship.

The captain and the second mate, in the other two boats, kept up the pursuit, and soon struck another whale. They being at this time a considerable distance to leeward, I went forward, braced around the main-yard, and put the ship off in a direction for them. The boat which had been stove was immediately hoisted in, and after examining the hole, I found that I could, by nailing a piece of canvas over it, get her ready to join in a fresh pursuit, sooner than by lowering down the other remaining boat which belonged to the ship. I accordingly turned her over upon the quarter, and was in the act of nailing on the canvas, when I observed a very large spermaceti whale, as well as I could judge, about eighty-five feet in length. He broke water about twenty rods off our weather bow, and was lying quietly, with his head in a direction for the ship. He spouted two or three times, and then disappeared. In less than two or three seconds he came up again, about the length of the ship off, and made directly for us, at the rate of about three knots. The ship was then going with about the same velocity. His appearance and attitude gave us at first no alarm; but while I stood watching his movements, and observing him but a ship's length off, coming down for us with great celerity, I involuntarily ordered the boy at the helm to put it hard up; intending

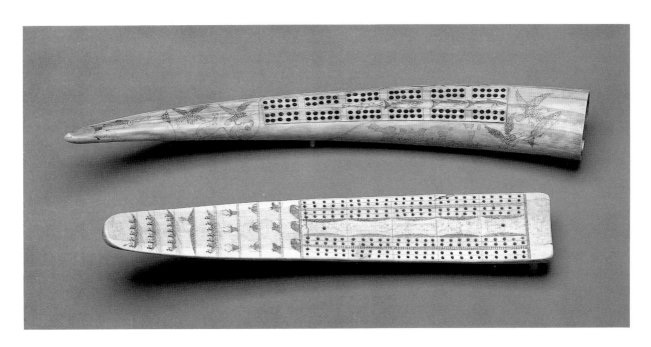

CRIBBAGE BOARDS MADE OF IVORY WALRUS TUSK

to sheer off and avoid him. The words were scarcely out of my mouth, before he came down upon us with full speed, and struck the ship with his head, just forward of the fore-chains; he gave us such an appalling and tremendous jar, as nearly threw us all on our faces. The ship brought up as suddenly and violently as if she had struck a rock, and trembled for a few seconds like a leaf. We looked at each other with perfect amazement, deprived almost of the power of speech. Many minutes elapsed before we were able to realize the dreadful accident, during which time he passed under the ship, grazing her keel as he went along, came up alongside of her to leeward, and lay on the top of the water (apparently stunned with the violence of the blow), for the space of a minute; he then suddenly started off, in a direction to leeward. After a few moments' reflection, and recovering, in some measure, from the sudden consternation that had seized us, I of course concluded that he had stove a hole in the ship, and that it would be necessary to set the pumps going. Accordingly they were rigged, but had not been in operation more than one minute, before I perceived the head of the ship to be gradually settling down in the water; I then ordered the signal to be set for the other boats, which, scarcely had

I despatched, before I again discovered the whale, apparently in convulsions, on the top of the water, about one hundred rods to leeward. He was enveloped in the foam of the sea, that his continual and violent thrashing about in the water had created around him, and I could distinctly see him smite his jaws together, as if distracted with rage and fury. He remained a short time in this situation, and then started off with great velocity, across the bows of the ship, to windward.

By this time the ship had settled down a considerable distance in the water, and I gave her up as lost. I however, ordered the pumps to be kept constantly going, and endeavored to collect my thoughts for the occasion. I turned to the boats, two of which we then had with the ship, with an intention of clearing them away, and getting all things ready to embark in them, if there should be no other resource left; and while my attention was thus engaged for a moment, I was aroused with the cry of a man at the hatchway, "Here he is—he is making for us again." I turned around, and saw him about one hundred rods directly ahead of us, coming down with apparently twice his ordinary speed, and to me at that moment, it appeared with tenfold fury and vengeance in his aspect. The surf flew in all directions about him, and his course towards us was marked by a white foam of a rod in width, which he made with the continual violent thrashing of his tail; his head was about half out of water, and in that way he came upon, and again struck the ship. I was in hopes when I descried him making for us, that by a dexterous movement of putting the ship away immediately, I should be able to cross the line of his approach, before he could get up to us, and thus avoid, what I knew, if he should strike us again, would prove our inevitable destruction. I bawled out to the helmsman, "hard up!" but she had not fallen off more than a point before we took the second shock. I should judge the speed of the ship to have been at this time about three knots, and that of the whale about six. He struck her to windward, directly under the cathead, and completely stove in her bows. He passed under the ship again, went off to leeward, and we saw no more of him.

Our situation at this juncture can be more readily imagined than described. The shock to our feelings was such, as I am sure none can have an adequate conception of, that were not there: the misfortune befell us at a moment when we least dreamt of any accident; and from the pleasing anticipations we had formed, of realizing the certain profits of our labor, we were dejected by a sudden, most mysterious, and overwhelming calamity. Not a moment, however, was to be lost in endeavoring to provide for the extremity to which it was now certain we were reduced. We were more than a thousand miles from the nearest land, and with nothing but a light open boat as the resource of safety for myself and companions. I ordered the men to cease pumping, and every one to provide for himself; seizing a hatchet at the same time, I cut away the lashings of the spare boat, which lay bottom up across two spars directly over the quarter deck, and cried out to those near me to take her as she came down. They did so accordingly, and bore her on their shoulders as far as the waist of the ship. The steward had in the mean time gone down into the cabin twice, and saved two quadrants, two practical navigators, and the captain's trunk and mine; all which were hastily thrown into the boat, as she lay on the deck, with the two compasses which I snatched from the binnacle. He attempted to descend again, but

A SHIP LYING AT ANCHOR IN THE HARBOR OF PUERTO MONTT, CHILE

A MID-NINETEENTH CENTURY SHIPYARD

the water by this time had rushed in, and he returned without being able to effect his purpose.

By the time we had got the boat to the waist, the ship had filled with water, and was going down on her beam-ends. We shoved our boat as quickly as possible from the plank-shear into the water, all hands jumping in her at the same time, and launched off clear of the ship. We were scarcely two boat's lengths distant from her, when she fell over to windward, and settled down in the water.

Amazement and despair now wholly took possession of us. We contemplated the frightful situation the ship lay in, and thought with horror upon the sudden and dreadful calamity that had overtaken us. We looked upon each other, as if to gather some consolatory sensation from an interchange of sentiments, but every countenance was marked with the paleness of despair. Not a word was spoken for several minutes by any of us; all appeared to be bound in a spell of stupid consternation; and from the time we were first attacked by the whale,

to the period of the fall of the ship, and of our leaving her in the boat, more than ten minutes could not certainly have elapsed! God only knows in what way, or by what means, we were enabled to accomplish in that short time what we did; the cutting away and transporting the boat from where she was deposited would of itself, in ordinary circumstances, have consumed as much time as that, if the whole ship's crew had been employed in it. My companions had not saved a single article but what they had on their backs; but to me it was a source of infinite satisfaction, if any such could be gathered from the horrors of our gloomy situation, that we had been fortunate enough to have preserved our compasses, navigators, and quadrants.

After the first shock of my feelings was over, I enthusiastically contemplated them as the probable instruments of our salvation; without them all would have been dark and hopeless. Gracious God! what a picture of distress and suffering now presented itself to my imagination. The crew of the ship were saved, consisting of twenty human souls. All that remained to conduct these twenty beings through the stormy terrors of the ocean, perhaps many thousand miles, were three open light boats. The prospect of obtaining any provisions or water from the ship, to subsist upon during the time, was at least now doubtful. How many long and watchful nights, thought I, are to be passed? How many tedious days of partial starvation are to be endured, before the least relief or mitigation of our sufferings can be reasonably anticipated?

We lay at this time in our boat, about two ship's lengths off from the wreck, in perfect silence, calmly contemplating her situation, and absorbed in our own melancholy reflections, when the other boats were discovered rowing up to us. They had but shortly before discovered that some accident had befallen us, but of the nature of which they were entirely ignorant. The sudden and mysterious disappearance of the ship was first discovered by the boatsteerer in the captain's boat, and with a horror-struck countenance and voice, he suddenly exclaimed, "Oh, my God! where is the ship?" Their operations upon this were instantly suspended, and a general cry of horror and despair burst from the lips of every man, as their looks were directed for her, in vain, over every part of the ocean. They immediately made all haste towards us.

The captain's boat was the first that reached us. He stopped about a boat's length off, but had no power to utter a single syllable: he was so completely overpowered with the spectacle before him, that he sat down in his boat, pale and speechless. I could scarcely recognize his countenance, he appeared to be so much altered, awed, and overcome, with the oppression of his feelings, and the dreadful reality that lay before him. He was in a short time however enabled to address the inquiry to me, "My God, Mr. Chase, what is the matter?" I answered, "We have been stove by a whale." I then briefly told him the story. After a few moments' reflection he observed that we must cut away her masts, and endeavor to get something out of her to eat. Our thoughts were now all accordingly bent on endeavors to save from the wreck whatever we might possibly want, and for this purpose we rowed up and got on to her. Search was made for every means of gaining access to her hold; and for this purpose the lanyards were cut loose, and with our hatchets we commenced to cut

away the masts, that she might right up again, and enable us to scuttle her decks. In doing which we were occupied about three quarters of an hour, owing to our having no axes, nor indeed any other instruments but the small hatchets belonging to the boats.

After her masts were gone she came up about two-thirds of the way upon an even keel. While we were employed about the masts the captain took his quadrant, shoved off from the ship, and got an observation. We found ourselves in latitude 0° 40' south longitude 119° west. We now commenced to cut a hole through the planks, directly above two large casks of bread, which most fortunately were between decks, in the waist of the ship, and which being in the upper side when she upset, we had strong hopes were not wet. It turned out according to our wishes, and from these casks we obtained six hundred pounds of hard bread. Other parts of the deck were then scuttled, and we got without difficulty as much freshwater as we dared to take in the boats, so that each was supplied with about sixty-five gallons. We got also from one of the lockers a musket, a small canister of powder, a couple of files, two rasps, about two pounds of boat nails, and a few turtle. In the afternoon the wind came on to blow a strong breeze, and having obtained every thing that occurred to us could then be got out, we began to make arrangements for our safety during the night.

A boat's line was made fast to the ship, and to the other end of it one of the boats was moored at about fifty fathoms to leeward. Another boat was then attached to the first one, about eight fathoms astern, and the third boat, the like distance astern of her. Night came on just as we had finished our operations; and such a night as it was to us! so full of feverish and distracting inquietude, that we were deprived entirely of rest. The wreck was constantly before my eyes. I could not, by any effort, chase away the horrors of the preceding day from my mind: they haunted me the live-long night. My companions—some of them were like sick women; they had no idea of the extent of their deplorable situation. One or two slept unconcernedly, while others wasted the night in unavailing murmurs. I now had full leisure to examine, with some degree of coolness, the dreadful circumstances of our disaster. The scenes of yesterday passed in such quick succession in my mind that it was not until after many hours of severe reflection that I was able to discard the idea of the catastrophe as a dream. Alas! it was one from which there was no awaking; it was too certainly true, that but yesterday we had existed as it were, and in one short moment had been cut off from all the hopes and prospects of the living! I have no language to paint out the horrors of our situation. To shed tears was indeed altogether unavailing, and withal unmanly; yet I was not able to deny myself the relief they served to afford me.

After several hours of idle sorrow and repining I began to reflect upon the accident, and endeavored to realize by what unaccountable destiny or design (which I could not at first determine), this sudden and most deadly attack had been made upon us: by an animal, too, never before suspected of premeditated violence, and proverbial for its insensibility and inoffensiveness. Every fact seemed to warrant me in concluding that it was anything but chance which directed his operations; he made two several attacks upon the ship, at a short interval between them, both of which, according to their direction, were calculated to do us the most injury, by being made ahead, and thereby combining the speed of the two objects for the shock; to effect which, the exact maneuvers which he made were necessary. His aspect was most horrible, and such as indicated resentment and fury. He came directly from the shoal which we had just before entered, and in which we had struck three of his companions, as if fired with revenge for their sufferings. But to this it may be observed, that the mode of fighting which they always adopt is either with repeated strokes of their tails, or snapping of their jaws together; and that a case, precisely similar to this one, has never been heard of amongst the oldest and most experienced whalers. To this I would answer, that the structure and the strength of the whale's head is admirably designed for this mode of attack; the most prominent part of which is almost as hard and as tough as iron. Indeed, I can compare it to nothing else but the inside of a horse's hoof, upon which a lance or a harpoon would not make the slightest impression. The eyes and the ears are removed nearly one-third the length of the whole fish from the front part of the head, and are not in the least degree endangered in this mode of attack. At all events, the whole circumstances taken together, all happening before my own eyes, and producing, at the time, impressions in my mind of decided, calculat-

ing mischief on the part of the whale (many of which impressions I cannot now recall), induce me to be satisfied that I am correct in my opinion. It is certainly, in all its bearings, a hitherto unheard of circumstance, and constitutes, perhaps, the most extraordinary one in the annals of the fishery.

In 1819, the American whaler Essex *sailed into the hunting grounds of the Pacific and was destroyed by an enraged sperm whale. This harrowing account by the ship's first mate of the whale's premeditated attack and the consequent helpless condition of the sailors provided the inspiration for Herman Melville's masterpiece,* Moby Dick.

Life at Sea

The Nautical School St. Marys

From *Harper's New Monthly Magazine, 1879*

"We propose, Sir, to teach a boy that the keel is somewhere, and that the keelson is not upon the spar deck"—an announcement which, in its sententious and semi-satirical vein, reminds one of Dr. Samuel Johnson, who might have uttered it had he been the expositor of a system of nautical education; but the speaker was Captain Erben, of the training ship *St. Marys*, in New York, and the occasion of the remark was a conversation on the *raison d'étre* of that school. Taken literally, the captain's statement would not indicate a very full curriculum; but epigram is never literal, and the prosaic basis of fact in this one was the object of the school to produce thorough sailors for the mercantile navy. The decline of American shipping has been attended by the disappearance of American sailors, whose places have been taken by Scandinavians, Germans, and Dutch. It is next to impossible to obtain a full crew of Americans for a large ship, and at the same time those who are available do not compare in discipline, experience, or intelligence with their foreign competitors. Now if it is remembered that a great trade upon the seas is never developed among a race of poor seamen, that good and numerous ships can not be of use without good and numerous men to man them, the reason why the school on board the *St. Marys* was opened will be apparent. At Annapolis the United States government maintains the superbly equipped Academy for the education of naval officers; and boys enlisting for service as foremast hands on war vessels are received on board certain United States ships, where they are subjected to a preparatory course. But until the *St. Marys* was opened the boy who had not the mathematical ability or the political influence to insure admission at Annapolis, nor the willingness to bind himself for a long term of service, with very slow advancement, on a warship—the son of a mechanic, clerk, or poor professional man, with a preference for the merchant navy—had no other beginning open to him than a berth as ordinary seaman on board any vessel that he could get. Shipping without any experience, his first voyage was likely to either brutalize him or to drive him to other occupations. His ignorance, so complete that he probably had no idea that the keelson was not a continuation of the jib boom, made him practically useless at the outset, and his uselessness was a pretext for the application of a rope's-end. Many and many a disgraceful incident, some within the writer's own observation, might be related of the mercilessness of captains and mates in dealing with greenhorns. Despite the agitation and legislation for the protec-

52

tion of seamen in recent years, a bully on the high seas is still defiant of law, and allows his ferocity full swing, finding immunity from reprisals in the laziness or indifference of consuls abroad to whom complaints are made, and at home in the indisposition of the sufferers to seek redress which involves costly legal proceedings. Unhappy the men under such a despot, and thrice unhappy the more helpless boys! Instances well authenticated in every particular are at the writer's hand of ordinarily well-behaved boys who, through the virulent ill will and the persistent abuse of their captains, have been driven to desert at distant ports, where, being left without any resources, they have been forever lost to their friends; and we remember an amiable boy, sensitive and delicate, who, having been severely beaten on the head by one of the mates, sprang overboard in delirium, with the curses of his persecutor for his burial rites. The lone empire of the sea, with its spacious solitude and sad gray boundaries, implants a sort of pathetic greatness in some men, while in others its sequestration from the amenities of the civilized earth encourages tyrannous and merciless license.

Even if the beginner had a humane captain and kindly shipmates considerate of his inexperience, his ignorance was sure to embitter his life until he could "learn the ropes." In English ships apprentices are taken, who are berthed apart from the crew, and are afforded an opportunity to observe the work of a ship before they are required to take part in it; and on the *St. Marys* it is possible for a boy before going to sea to know that "the keel is somewhere, and that the keelson is not upon the spar deck."

Having cognizance of the necessity of a change in the then existing circumstances, some prominent merchants, underwriters, and shipowners obtained an act from the New York Legislature, about six years ago, authorizing the Board of Education to provide a nautical school for the training of pupils in the science of navigation and the practical duties of mariners, and to secure from the United States government the use of a vessel for the purpose. The control of the school was placed in five Commissioners of Education and three members of the Chamber of Commerce. The government loaned the sloop of war the *St. Marys*, under an act of Congress approved June 2, 1874, which extended similar privileges to other ports, as follows: That, to promote nautical education, the Secretary of the Navy is empowered to furnish, upon the application in writing of the Governor of a State, a suitable vessel of the navy, with all her apparel, charts, books, and instruments of navigation, provided the same can be spared without detriment to the naval service, for the instruction of youths in navigation, seamanship, marine enginery, and all matters pertaining to the proper construction, equipment, and sailing of vessels; and the President is authorized to detail proper officers of the navy as superintendents and instructors in such schools.

Besides New York, San Francisco availed itself of the enactment; but the *Jamestown* being loaned to that city, the vessel was returned to the government last winter after an unsuccessful experiment, and the *St. Marys* is now the only nautical school existing under the law.

The preparation of a suitable code was a difficult matter. A good class of scholars was sought—superior to those who would enter the naval training ships; and as the school was tentative, it was thought best to impose as few restrictions as possible upon them. For this reason the duration of his stay has been left to the option of the scholar; and though the course is for two years, he may retire at any time. Candidates for admission must not be under fifteen years of age nor over twenty, and they must be of a sound constitution, and free from all physical defects. They must evince some aptitude or inclination for sea life, and bring with them a certificate of good moral character. Previous to the opening of the nautical school, a school-ship for the reformation of juvenile offenders was stationed in the harbor, and the former has been confounded with the latter, which is no longer in existence, but the fact of the matter is that no one who has been convicted of a crime can be admitted on board the *St. Marys*, and boys of evil disposition are not retained. Successful candidates are received at any time. They are required to bring with them two pairs of boots, three towels, three pairs of heavy socks, three pairs of heavy drawers, three heavy undershirts, three pocket-handkerchiefs, various brushes, combs, and the odds and ends for repairing that are always found in a sailor's ditty bag. Two suits of clothes, caps, a hammock, and blankets are provided by the ship, and charged against a deposit of thirty-five dollars made when the scholar enters, and except the trifling cost of replacing or repairing boots and underwear, this sum covers all the expenses of a two years' course on board the *St. Marys*. If at the end of his first year a boy engages to continue his studies throughout the second year, the charges against him are wiped out, and the whole amount of his original deposit is again placed to his credit. Few institutions are established on a more liberal basis, or offer so favorable an opportunity for obtaining a common-school education combined with a practical knowledge of the duties of a seaman; but unless a boy has fully made up his mind to be a sailor, and has the physical strength to endure certain hardships, the nautical school is not the place for him, and time spent there will be fruitless. During the winter the ship is stationed at the foot of Twenty-third Street, East River, and boys whose behavior has been good are allowed to spend Saturday afternoon and Sunday with their parents or relatives, if the latter are resident in or near the city. If their guardians are not in the city, they are required to sleep on board the ship, and their leave of absence is suspended or abridged in proportion to the degree of their misconduct during the week.

The *St. Marys* is a sloop of war, which, though she is thirty-three years old, is still stanch and fast. She registers about one thousand tons, and her full armament is sixteen 18-inch guns. Her officers are: Superintendent, Commander Henry Erben; Executive, Lieutenant-Commander J.J. Hunker; Instructors, Lieutenant A.P. Osborn, Lieutenant Robert G. Peck, and Acting Assistant Surgeon J.J. Page. All these gentlemen belong to the United States Navy, and their services are provided by the general government gratuitously.

It is probable, we suppose, that the boy who has made up his mind to be a sailor has learned something about ships by reading and observation, that his weather eye is open, and that when he steps up the gangplank of the *St. Marys* for the first time he feels more like an admiral than a greenhorn. Boyish fancies are so strange that the gun deck may appear pleasanter to him than the little parlor at home. And let us hope that such fancies will smooth down many of the things that would jar upon him if he were less enamored with his future profession. His private clothing is cast aside for a uniform, consisting of a dress suit of blue, and a working suit of white canvas. The dress suit consists of blue trousers, a blue cap with gold lettering, and a blue shirt with a wide collar and white braiding. Ten to one he looks brighter, stronger, and altogether more shipshape in these than the garments which he discards, no matter how fashionable or fine they may be. He is classified and quartered according to his size, age, and general abilities. The boys are divided into two watches, and the watches are divided into crews, each crew having sixteen boys, in the charge of an experienced seaman, who teaches them the duties of a sailor. The beginner has a number, a crew, a mess, and a watch. What wonder if he hitches his trousers with unnecessary frequency, walks with a rolling motion expressive of tempestuous seas, and stands with his legs apart in the most approved style of the ideal Jack Tar! It is easy for him to forget that he is alongside of a city wharf: his companions talk a nautical slang, the ship's bell strikes the half hours and hours—a clock is never thought of—and the bread served with dinner is old-fashioned "hardtack." The illusion is further sustained by these very difficult biscuits, which, having been the almost exclusive food of sailors in all the romances he has read, are more palatable to him than the creamiest Vienna or the softest and sweetest French bread. Perhaps a morsel opens a train of retrospective to him, in which he sees shipwrecked mariners adrift on rafts in blood-red southern seas, with one biscuit between them and complete starvation. The imagination of boyhood is swift, and "takes suggestion as a cat laps milk." When bedtime is "piped" he swings his hammock, and if he is extremely "fresh," it is probable that he fancies he has stood a watch at sea on a stormy night, and is turning in with wet garments. His slumbers are sweetened by the thought, and sleep folds in her arms not a callow lad, but a grizzled, sunburned, dripping seaman. The dream is grotesquely and suddenly dispelled. Two young conspirators in airy dress steal softly up to him, and a sheath knife is seen to gleam as that plebeian weapon usually gleams in melodramas and the stories of the *Weekly Wash-Tub*. The cords suspending the hammock are cut, and in a moment the dreamer is awake, prostrate on the deck, with only the fluttering tail of a retreating garment in sight to tell him that all the other boys are not as fast asleep as the heaviness of their breathing would lead one to suppose. Thus begin the tribulations that are to break in upon his dreams more than once, and to disillusion him, until, in old manhood or sooner, he learns how uncom-

PRIVATE FLAGS OF SHIPOWNERS AND MERCHANTS OF THE PORT OF NEW YORK

A MODEL OF A 1908 LIGHTSHIP

fortable a profession he has chosen. Hazing in its more serious forms is prevented, and that which does not severely injure the victim is neither countenanced nor suppressed.

All hands are sharply called at six o'clock in the morning, or "four bells," the hammocks are lashed and stowed away, the decks are swept, and at seven o'clock each boy is expected to appear at inspection with a clean face and hands and smoothly brushed hair. Meanwhile the berth deck is pervaded with the grateful odor of tea, coffee, mush, and fresh bread. The galley is "for'ard," and the cook is busy with the large simmering coffee kettles that surround him. The portable ta-

bles are "shipped," which means, in the vernacular of the sea, that they are placed in position, and at half past seven breakfast is served, under the supervision of the master-at-arms. The boys in the mess act as its cook in rotation. The incumbent washes all dishes, brings the food from the galley, and apportions it; and if anyone is dissatisfied with his own plate, he may demand an exchange with the cook. Between eight o'clock, when breakfast is finished, and nine, the cooks scour the dishes and tables, while the others clean up the decks, sweeping or holystoning them according to the day. At nine the executive officer scrutinizes the mess gear, which is spread out for his inspection, and after a lesson from the Bible has been read, the academic exercises of the day are begun, and continued until half past eleven.

The course includes reading, writing, spelling, geography, arithmetic, and English grammar. This part savors too much of the shore to be appreciated; it is prosaic, and our new boy is apt to consider it irksome. But the exercises in seamanship, the making of knots, hitches, and bends of wonderfully varied and unaccountable nomenclature, sail mending and sail bending, are entered upon with zeal and pleasure. Should you ask the new boy the name of the smallest rope with the longest name, he would probably be able to glibly tell you, at the end of his first month on board, that it is the "starboard-foretop-gallant-studding-sail-boom-tricing-line-block-strap-thimble-seizing;" and in a short time he becomes a master of the conundrums which old salts have invented for the mystification of young ones. He can tell you what is forward on the starboard side, aft on the port side, and inside on the outside; how to pass a nipper, or clap on a jigger; how to choke a luff, or snake the backstays; how to fleet a purchase, or crown a crotch rope; how to make a grommet or an artificial eye; how to make a Spanish fox or a Turk's head; and the meaning of a withe, a gammoning, a cat's-paw, a sheepshank, an Irish splice, the whiskers, the jumpers, a cock's comb, a gasket, a tripshaw, a camel, a Flemish hare, and a ring-tail—all these being nautical terms. He can name every sail above the skysail on the most preposterously overweighted clipper—the moon sails, stargazers, skyscrapers, and heaven-disturbers. His education includes the whole catalogue of hitches, bends, clinches, hawsers, and splices: the clove hitch, the timber hitch, the Blackwall hitch, the rolling hitch, and two half hitches; the sheet bend and the curricle bend; the inside clinch and the outside clinch; the carrick bend, the marline hitch, and the kackling. Weather forecasts are put in rhyme for him, and from constant repetition become indelibly impressed upon his memory:

A red sky in the morning,
Sailors, take warning;
A red sky at night
Is a sailor's delight.

The evening red, the morning gray,
Are sure signs of a fine day;
But the evening gray and morning red

Make the sailor shake his head.
If the mist comes o'er the open sea,
Then fair weather, shipmate, it will be;
But if the mist comes off the land,
Then rain comes pouring o'er the strand.

With the rain before the wind,
Your topsail sheets and halyards mind;
But when the wind's before the rain,
You may hoist your topsails up again.

The printed questions put to him at the examinations cover about fifty pages as large as these of *Harper's Magazine*. He learns how to scull, row, steer, and sail a boat; how to box the compass, steer by the compass, and take compass bearings; how to heave the lead; how to swim; and how to bend, loosen, furl, and reef a sail. The instruction in navigation embraces the working of a day's reckoning, the use of the quadrant and sextant, the finding of latitude and longitude, and the mode of keeping a log. It is not intended to graduate officers, but if a boy takes advantage of all the opportunities open to him on board the *St. Marys*, he may, after his first or second post-graduate voyage, immediately qualify for the position of mate.

The recitations and exercises of the morning are closed at half past eleven, and recreation is allowed from then until dinnertime—an hour later. The dinner consists of soup, fresh meat, vegetables, and "hardtack," served not in separate courses, but in one dish. The quality is good, and the quantity ample. From one o'clock until half past one all hands are occupied in cleaning decks, etc., and at half past one the school exercises are resumed. Most of the boys are less proficient in the English branches than others of a corresponding age in the public schools, but a few are so far advanced that navigation is substituted for other studies. While we were on board, one of the instructors gave Autobiography as a subject for a twenty minutes' composition, and as indicating the cleverness in the class and the social position of some of the scholars, we selected the following, which was written in a legible hand, with correct punctuation:

Your humble servant, the author, was born on the first day of March, 1861. Of his past life little can be

SCRIMSHAW, THE WHALER'S ART, ON A SPERM WHALE TOOTH

While there are some boys of good birth and education on board the ship, there are others rough, vulgar, and illiterate; but the moral and social standing of the nautical school is quite as high as that of any public school. The misapprehension upon this point to which we have referred, arising from a confusing of the reformatory ship *Mercury* and the *St. Marys*, led Captain Erben to say that the latter should be named and numbered as a public school; but we believe he did not foresee that such a change might cause still greater misapprehension should a bucolic reader find in his newspaper the announcement that Public School No. 90 (for instance) had returned from an Atlantic cruise of five months!

The school exercises of the day end at four o'clock. A supper of tea or coffee, with fresh bread and butter, is served at five o'clock; and until nine o'clock, when "turn in" is piped, a few simple duties and recreations occupy the time. The berth deck is warm and comfortable. There is a piano, which never lacks performers during the hours of recreation, and there is a model printing press, and a small collection of good secular books. Smoking is not forbidden; some urchins may be seen puffing away at their pipes as though they fully appreciated the charms of the habit. The high spirits and athletic capabilities of the boys are developed in "skylarking"—not the mundane antics of boys ashore, but the daredeviltry afloat that gives the word its significance. Occasionally a reception is held; the gun deck is cleared, and draped with bunting, a band is hired from the city, and partners are selected from the invited company of pretty girls. But the event of the year is the annual cruise, when the ship leaves her wharf at Twenty-third Street, and sails to Lisbon or some other pleasant port, calling *en route* at the Azores, Madeira, or the Bermudas. Arithmetic, grammar, and all other such prosaic studies and textbooks are then abandoned, and all

said that differs radically from the career of thousands of others. He was led into the same errors, beset by the same temptations and petty follies that harass all other young men. His father enlisted in the navy during the war and remained in the service till 1870. This made a constant change of base necessary for the family economy, and consequently the author has resided in various cities throughout the Union, and changed his instructors and textbooks so often that he is somewhat backward in his studies, and his knowledge is much confused and various. He has spent his life in comparative ease under a stern but kind discipline, doing but little manual labor, except for amusement. Most of his time was spent in study and the perusal of popular scientific books. This inactive life has produced its full amount of laziness and constitutional fatigue. It is not known that any thing remarkable ever happened to him, except, perhaps, a narrow escape from drowning which he was led into by his taste for the water. He is not quite certain what kind of a man he would like to become. This question was always a difficult one for young men to solve, and he has not decided whether he would rather go to sea, or be a tramp.

J. J. W.

NEW YORK'S UPPER BAY IN THE 1850S

the time is given to practical seamanship and naviga-tion. The boys work the ship, with the assistance of six sailors; they stand their watches, take their turn at the wheel, and are required to go aloft in all sorts of weath-er. This tests their mettle, and some of them come to the conclusion that the writers of nautical novels are heartless impostors. At the end of the cruise the annual examination is held, and the graduates, to whom a handsome parchment certificate is awarded, with the addition of one silver and two bronze medals to the three most proficient, usually find no difficulty in ob-taining a berth on a good ship.

The *St. Marys* now has about one hundred boys aboard, and can accommodate nearly as many more. We believe that she is a great benefit to the city, and an ad-vantage to the mercantile service of the country. That she is a success is largely due to the zealous support given by the chairman of the Nautical School Commit-tee of the Board of Education, Mr. David R. Wetmore, who has been untiring in his efforts among his col-leagues, and without whom the school would have probably been discontinued some time ago.

His First Voyage

Herman Melville

The second day out of port, the decks being washed down and breakfast over, the watch was called, and the mate set us to work.

It was a very bright day. The sky and water were both of the same deep hue, and the air felt warm and sunny, so that we threw off our jackets. I could hardly believe that I was sailing in the same ship I had been in during the night, when everything had been so lonely and dim; and I could hardly imagine that this was the same ocean, now so beautiful and blue, that during part of the night watch had rolled along so black and forbidding.

There were little traces of sunny clouds all over the heavens, and little fleeces of foam all over the sea; and the ship made a strange, musical noise under her bows, as she glided along with her sails all still. It seemed a pity to go to work at such a time, and if we could only have sat in the windlass again, or if they would have let me go out on the bowsprit, and lay down between the *manropes* there, and look over at the fish in the water, and think of home, I should have been almost happy for a time.

I had now completely got over my sea-sickness, and felt very well, at least in my body, though my heart was far from feeling right, so that I could now look around me and make observations.

And truly, though we were at sea, there was much to behold and wonder at, to me, who was on my first voyage. What most amazed me was the sight of the great ocean itself, for we were out of sight of land. All round us, on both sides of the ship, ahead and astern, nothing was to be seen but water—water—water; not a single glimpse of green shore, not the smallest island, or speck of moss anywhere. Never did I realize till now what the ocean was: how grand and majestic, how solitary, and boundless, and beautiful and blue; for that day it gave no tokens of squalls or hurricanes, such as I had heard my father tell of; nor could I imagine how anything that seemed so playful and placid could be lashed into rage, and troubled into rolling avalanches of foam, and great cascades of waves, such as I saw in the end.

As I looked at it so mild and sunny, I could not help calling to my mind my little brother's face when he was sleeping, an infant in the cradle. It had just such a happy, careless, innocent look; and every happy little wave seemed gambolling about like a thoughtless little kid in a pasture, and seemed to look up in your face as it passed, as if it wanted to be patted and caressed. They seemed all live things with hearts in them, that could feel; and I almost felt grieved as we sailed in among them, scattering them under our broad bows in sunflakes, and riding over them like a great elephant among lambs.

But what seemed perhaps the most strange to me of all was a certain wonderful rising and falling of the sea; I do not mean the waves themselves, but a sort of wide heaving and swelling and sinking all over the ocean. It was something I cannot very well describe; but I know very well what it was, and how it affected me. It made me almost dizzy to look at it, and yet I could not keep my eyes off it, it seemed so passing strange and wonderful.

I felt as if in a dream all the time; and when I could shut the ship out, almost thought I was in some new, fairy world, and expected to hear myself called to, out of the clear blue air, or from the depths of the deep blue sea. But I did not have much leisure to indulge in such thoughts, for the men were now getting some *stun' sails* ready to hoist aloft, as the wind was getting fairer and fairer for us; and these stun' sails are light canvas which are spread at such times, away out beyond the ends of the yards, where they overhang the wide water like the wings of a great bird.

For my own part I could do but little to help the rest, not knowing the name of anything or the proper way to go about aught. Besides, I felt very dreamy, as I said before, and did not exactly know where or what I was, everything was so strange and new.

While the stun' sails were lying all tumbled upon the deck, and the sailors were fastening them to the booms, getting them ready to hoist, the mate ordered me to do a great many simple things, none of which could I comprehend, owing to the queer words he used; and then, seeing me stand quite perplexed and confounded, he would roar out at me, and call me all manner of names, and the sailors would laugh and wink to each other, but durst not go farther than that for fear of the mate, who in his own presence would not let any body laugh at me but himself.

However, I tried to wake up as much as I could, and keep from dreaming with my eyes open; and being, at bottom, a smart, apt lad, at last I managed to learn a thing or two, so that I did not appear so much like a fool as at first.

People who have never gone to sea for the first time as sailors cannot imagine how puzzling and confounding it is. It must be like going into a barbarous country where they speak a strange dialect, and dress in strange clothes, and live in strange houses. For sailors have their own names, even for things that are familiar ashore; and if you call a thing by its shore name, you are laughed at for an ignoramus and a landlubber. This first day I speak of, the mate having ordered me to draw some water, I asked him where I was to get the pail, when I thought I had committed some dreadful crime, for he flew into a great passion and said they never had any *pails* at sea, and then I learned that they were always called *buckets*. And once I was talking about sticking a little wooden peg into a bucket to stop a leak, when he flew out again, and said there were no *pegs* at sea, only *plugs*. And just so it was with everything else.

But besides all this, there is such an infinite number of totally new names of new things to learn, that at first it seemed impossible for me to master them all. If you have ever seen a ship, you must have remarked what a thicket of ropes there are, and how they all seemed mixed and entangled together like a great skein of yarn. Now the very smallest of these ropes has its own proper name, and many of them are very lengthy, like the names of young royal princes, such as the *starboard-main-topgallant-bowline*, or the *larboard-fore-topsail-clue-line*.

I think it would not be a bad plan to have a grand new naming of a ship's ropes, as I have read, they once had a simplifying of the classes of plants in botany. It is really wonderful how many names there are in the world. There is no counting the names that surgeons and anatomists give to the various parts of the human body, which, indeed, is something like a ship, its bones being the stiff standing rigging, and the sinews the small running ropes, that manage all the motions.

I wonder whether mankind could not get along without all these names, which keep increasing every day, and hour, and moment, till at last the very air will be full of them; and even in a great plain, men will be breathing each other's breath, owing to the vast multitude of words they use that consume all the air, just as lamp-burners do gas. But people seem to have a great love for names, for to know a great many names seems to look like knowing a good many things; though I

ABOVE: NEW YORK'S EAST RIVER WATERFRONT C. 1900
LEFT: CLIPPER SHIP CARDS ADVERTISING FOR CARGOES AND PASSENGERS

should not be surprised if there were a great many more names than things in the world. But I must quit this rambling and return to my story.

At last we hoisted the stun' sails up to the topsail yards, and as soon as the vessel felt them she gave a sort of bound like a horse, and the breeze blowing more and more, she went plunging along, shaking off the foam from her bows like foam from a bridle bit. Every mast and timber seemed to have a pulse in it that was beating with life and joy, and I felt a wild exulting in my own heart, and felt as if I would be glad to bound along so round the world.

Then was I first conscious of a wonderful thing in me, that responded to all the wild commotion of the outer world, and went reeling on and on with the planets in their orbits and was lost in one delirious throb at the center of the All. A wild bubbling and bursting was at my heart, as if a hidden spring had just gushed out there, and my blood ran tingling along my frame like mountain brooks in spring freshets.

Yes! yes! give me this glorious ocean life, this salt-sea life, this briny, foamy-life, when the sea neighs and snorts, and you breathe the very breath that the great whales respire! Let me roll around the globe, let me rock upon the sea, let me race and pant out my life with an eternal breeze astern and an endless sea before!

But how soon these raptures abated, when, after a brief idle interval, we were again set to work, and I had a vile commission to clean out the chicken coops and make up the beds of the pigs in the longboat.

Miserable dog's life is this of the sea! Commanded like a slave, and set to work like an ass! Vulgar and brutal men lording it over me, as if I were an African in Alabama. Yes, yes, blow on, ye breezes, and make a speedy end to this abominable voyage!

Herman Melville (1819–1891) went to sea at age twenty on an American merchant ship. He jumped ship, was captured by the Typees, reputed cannibals, and then roamed the South Pacific Islands. After being rescued, he took part in a ship mutiny, went to jail in Tahiti, and escaped. After his return to the United States, he wrote now immortalized stories of the sea, including the classic Moby Dick *(1851). This story is from his novel,* Redburn *(1849).*

Ambitious Jimmy Hicks

John Masefield

"Well," said the captain of the foretop to me, "it's our cutter today, and you're the youngest hand, and you'll be bowman. Can you pull an oar?" "No," I answered. "Well, you'd better pull one today, my son, or mind your eye. You'll climb Zion's Hill tonight if you go catching any crabs." With that he went swaggering along the deck, chewing his quid of sweet-cake. I thought lugubriously of Zion's Hill, a very different place from the one in the Bible, and the longer I thought, the chillier came the sweat on my palms. "Away cutters," went the pipe a moment later. "Down to your boat foretopmen." I skidded down the gangway into the bows of the cutter, and cast the turns from the painter, keeping the boat secured by a single turn. A strong tide was running, and the broken water was flying up in spray. Dirty water ran in trickles down my sleeves. The thwarts were wet. A lot of dirty water was slopping about in the well. "Bowman," said the captain of the foretop, "why haven't you cleaned your boat out?" "I didn't know I had to." "Well, next time you don't know we'll jolly well duck you in it. Let go forward. Back a stroke, starboard. Down port, and shove her off." "Where are we going?" asked the stroke. "We're going to the etceteraed slip to get the etceteraed love-letters. Now look alive in the bows there.

Get your oars out and give way. If I come forward with the tiller your heads'll ache for a week." I got out my oar, or rather I got out the oar which had been left to me. It was one of the midship oars, the longest and heaviest in the boat. With this I made a shift to pull till we neared the slip, when I had to lay my oar in, gather up the painter, and stand by to leap on to the jetty to make the boat fast as we came alongside. I have known some misery in my time, but the agony of that moment, wondering if I should fall headlong on the slippery green weed, in the sight of the old sailors smoking there, was as bitter as any I have suffered. The cutter's nose rubbed the dangling seaweed. I made a spring, slipped, steadied myself, cast the painter around the mooring hook, and made the boat fast. "A round turn and two half hitches," I murmured, as I passed the turns, "and a third half hitch for luck." "Come off with your third half hitch," said one of the old sailors. "You and your three half hitches. You're like Jimmy Hicks, the come-day go-day. You want to do too much, you do. You'd go dry the keel with a towel, wouldn't you, rather than take a caulk? Come off with your third hitch."

Late that night I saw the old sailor in the lamp room cleaning the heavy copper lamps. I asked if I might help him, for I wished to hear the story of

64

Jimmy Hicks. He gave me half a dozen lamps to clean, with a mass of cotton waste and a few rags, most of them the relics of our soft cloth working caps. "Heave round, my son," he said "and get an appetite for your supper." When I had cleaned two or three of my lamps I asked him to tell me about Jimmy Hicks.

"Ah," he said, "you want to be warned by him. You're too ambitious altogether. Look at you coming here to clean my lamps. And you after pulling in the cutter. I wouldn't care to be like Jimmy Hicks. No. I wouldn't that. It's only young fellies like you wants to be like Jimmy Hicks." "Who was Jimmy Hicks?" I asked; "and what was it he did?"

"Ah," said the old man, "did you ever hear tell of the Black Ball Line? Well, there's no ships like them ships now. You think them Cunarders at the buoy there; you think them fine. You should a seen the *Red Jacket*, or the *John James Green*, or the *Thermopylae*. By dad, that *was* a sight. Spars—talk of spars. And skysail yards on all three masts, and a flying jib boom the angels could have picked their teeth with. Sixty-six days they took, the Thames to Sydney Heads. It's never been done before nor since. Well, Jimmy Hicks he was a young, ambitious felly, the same as you. And he was in one of them ships. I was shipmates with him myself.

"Well, of all the redheaded ambitious fellies I think Jimmy Hicks was the worst. Yes, sir. I think he was the worst. The day they got to sea the bosun set him to scrub the fo'c'sle. So he gets some sand and holystone and a three-cornered scraper, and he scrubs that fo'c'sle fit for an admiral. He begun that job at three bells in the morning watch, and he was doing it at eight bells, and half his watch below he was doing it, and when they called him for dinner he was still doing it. Talk about white. White was black alongside them planks. So in the afternoon it came on to blow. Yes, sir, it breezed up. So they had to snug her down. So Jimmy Hicks he went up and made the skysails fast, and then he made the royals fast. And then he come down to see had he got a good furl on them. And then up he went again and put a new stow on the skysail. And then he went up again to tinker the main royal bunt. Them furls of his, by dad, they reminded me of Sefton Park. Yes, sir; they was that like Sunday clothes.

"He was always like that. He wasn't never happy unless he was putting whippings on ropes' ends, or pointing the topgallant and royal braces, or polishing the brass on the ladders till it was as bright as gold. Always doing something. Always doing more than his piece. The last to leave the deck and the first to come up when hands were called. If he was told to whip a rope, he pointed it and gave it a rub of slush and Flemish-coiled it. If he was told to broom down the top of a deckhouse he got it white with a holystone. He was like the poet—

Double, double, toil and trouble.—Shakespeare. That was Jimmy Hicks. Yes, sir, that was him. You want to be warned by him. You hear the terrible end he come to.

"Now they was coming home in that ship. And what do you suppose they had on board? Well, they had silks. My word they was silks. Light as muslin. Worth a pound a fathom. All yellow and blue and red. All the colors. And a gloss. It was like so much moonlight. Well. They had a lot of that. Then they had china tea, and it wasn't none of your skilly. No, sir. It was tea the King of Spain could have drunk in the golden palaces of Rome. There was flaviour. Worth eighteen shilling a pound that tea was. The same as the Queen drunk. It was like meat that tea was. You didn't want no meat if you had a cup of that. Worth two hundred thousand pound that ship's freight was. And a general in the army was a passenger. Besides a bishop.

"So as they were coming home they got caught in a cyclone, off of the Mauritius. Whoo! You should a heard the wind. O mommer, it just blew. And the cold green seas they kept coming aboard. Ker-woosh, they kept coming. And the ship she groaned and she strained, and she worked her planking open. So it was all hands to the pumps, general and bishop and all, and they kept pumping out tea, all ready made with salt water. That was all they had to live on for three days. Salt-water tea. Very wholesome it is, too, for them that like it. *And* for them that's inclined to consumption.

"By and by the pumps choked. 'The silks is in the well,' said the mate. 'To your prayers, boys. We're gone up.' 'Hold on with prayers,' said the old man. 'Get a tackle rigged and hoist the boat out. You can pray afterwards. Work is prayer,' he says, 'so long as I command.' 'Lively there,' says the mate. 'Up there one of you with a block. Out to the mainyard arm and rig a tackle! Lively now. Stamp and go. She's settling under us.' So Jimmy Hicks seizes a tackle and they hook it on to the

65

THE AMERICAN CLIPPER SHIP, *REYNARD*, BUILT IN 1851

longboat, and Jimmy nips into the rigging with one of the blocks in his hand. And they clear it away to him as he goes. And she was settling like a stone all the time. 'Look slippy there, you!' cries the mate, as Jimmy lays out on the yard, for the sea was crawling across the deck. It was time to be gone out of that.

"And Jimmy gets to the yardarm, and he takes a round turn with his lashing, and he makes a half hitch, and he makes a second half hitch. 'Yardarm, there!' hails the mate. 'May we hoist away?' 'Hold on,' says Jimmy, 'till I make her fast,' he says. And just as he makes his third half hitch and yells to them to sway away—Ker-woosh! there comes a great green sea. And down they all go—ship, and tea, and mate, and bishop, and general, and Jimmy, and the whole lash-up. All the whole lot of them. And all because he would wait to take the third half hitch. So you be warned by Jimmy Hicks, my son. And don't you be neither redheaded nor ambitious."

Orphaned at the age of seven, John Masefield (1878–1967) ran away from relatives and at thirteen went to sea on a merchant training vessel. This story, from A Tarpaulin Muster *(1907), has a lesson: perfection has no place in a crisis.*

THE SIDE-WHEEL STEAMSHIP *WESTERN METROPOLIS*

"Blow Up with the Brig!"

by Wilkie Collins

I have got an alarming confession to make. I am haunted by a ghost.

If you were to guess for a hundred years, you would never guess what my ghost is. I shall make you laugh to begin with—and afterward I shall make your flesh creep. My ghost is the ghost of a bedroom candlestick.

Yes, a bedroom candlestick and candle, or a flat candlestick and candle—put it which way you like—that is what haunts me. I wish it was something pleasanter and more out of the common way; a beautiful lady, or a mine of gold and silver, or a cellar of wine and a coach and horses, and such like. But, being what it is, I must take it for what it is, and make the best of it; and I shall thank you kindly if you will help me out by doing the same.

I am not a scholar myself, but I make bold to believe that the haunting of any man with any thing under the sun begins with the frightening of him. At any rate, the haunting of me with a bedroom candlestick and candle began with the frightening of me with a bedroom candlestick and candle—the frightening of me half out of my life; and, for the time being, the frightening of me altogether out of my wits. That is not a very pleasant thing to confess before stating the particulars; but perhaps you will be the readier to believe that I am not a downright coward, because

you find me bold enough to make a clean breast of it already, to my own great disadvantage so far.

Here are the particulars, as well as I can put them:

I was apprenticed to the sea when I was about as tall as my own walking stick; and I made good enough use of my time to be fit for a mate's berth at the age of twenty-five years.

It was in the year eighteen hundred and eighteen, or nineteen, I am not quite certain which, that I reached the before-mentioned age of twenty-five. You will please to excuse my memory not being very good for dates, names, numbers, places, and such like. No fear, though, about the particulars I have undertaken to tell you of; I have got them all shipshape in my recollection; I can see them, at this moment, as clear as noonday in my own mind. But there is a mist over what went before, and, for the matter of that, a mist likewise over much that came after—and it's not very likely to lift at my time of life, is it?

Well, in eighteen hundred and eighteen, or nineteen, when there was peace in our part of the world—and not before it was wanted, you will say—there was fighting, of a certain scampering, scrambling kind, going on in that old battlefield which we seafaring men know by the name of the Spanish Main.

The possessions that belonged

to the Spaniards in South America had broken into open mutiny and declared for themselves years before. There was plenty of bloodshed between the new Government and the old; but the new had got the best of it, for the most part, under one General Bolivar—a famous man in his time, though he seems to have dropped out of people's memories now. Englishmen and Irishmen with a turn for fighting, and nothing particular to do at home, joined the general as volunteers; and some of our merchants here found it a good venture to send supplies across the ocean to the popular side. There was risk enough, of course, in doing this; but where one speculation of the kind succeeded, it made up for two, at the least, that failed. And that's the true principle of trade, wherever I have met with it, all the world over.

Among the Englishmen who were concerned in this Spanish-America business, I, your humble servant, happened, in a small way, to be one.

I was then mate of a brig belonging to a certain firm in the City, which drove a sort of general trade, mostly in queer out-of-the-way places, as far from home as possible; and which freighted the brig, in the year I am speaking of, with a cargo of gunpowder for General Bolivar and his volunteers. Nobody knew anything about our instructions, when we sailed, except the captain; and he didn't half seem to like them. I can't rightly say how many barrels of powder we had on board, or how much each barrel held—I only know we had no other cargo. The name of the brig was the *Good Intent*—a queer name enough, you will tell me, for a vessel laden with gunpowder, and sent to help a revolution. And as far as this particular voyage was concerned, so it was. I mean that for a joke, and I hope you will encourage me by laughing at it.

The *Good Intent* was the craziest tub of a vessel I ever went to sea in, and the worst found in all respects. She was two hundred and thirty, or two hundred and eighty tons burden, I forget which; and she had a crew of eight, all told—nothing like as many as we ought by rights to have had to work the brig. However, we were well and honestly paid our wages; and we had to set that against the chance of foundering at sea, and, on this occasion, likewise the chance of being blown up into the bargain.

In consideration of the nature of our cargo, we were harassed with new regulations, which we didn't at all like, relative to smoking our pipes and lighting our lanterns; and as usual in such cases, the captain, who made the regulations, preached what he didn't practice. Not a man of us was allowed to have a bit of lighted candle in his hand when he went below—except the skipper; and he used his light, when he turned in, or when he looked over his charts on the cabin table, just as usual.

This light was a common kitchen candle or "dip," and it stood in an old battered flat candlestick, with all the japan worn and melted off, and all the tin showing through. It would have been more seaman-like and suitable in every respect if he had had a lamp or a lantern; but he stuck to his old candlestick; and that same old candlestick has ever afterward stuck to *me*. That's another joke, if you please, and a better one than the first, in my opinion.

Well (I said "well" before, but it's a word that helps a man on like), we sailed in the brig, and shaped our course, first, for the Virgin Islands, in the West Indies; and, after sighting them, we made for the Leeward Islands next, and then stood on due south, till the lookout at the masthead hailed the deck and said he saw land. That land was the coast of South America. We had had a wonderful voyage so far. We had lost none of our spars or sails, and not a man of us had been harassed to death at the pumps. It wasn't often the *Good Intent* made such a voyage as that, I can tell you.

I was sent aloft to make sure about the land, and I did make sure of it.

When I reported the same to the skipper, he went below and had a look at his letter of instructions and the chart. When he came on deck again, he altered our course a trifle to the eastward—I forget the point on the compass, but that don't matter. What I do remember is, that it was dark before we closed in with the land. We kept the lead going, and hove the brig to in from four to five fathoms water, or it might be six—I can't say for certain. I kept a sharp eye to the drift of the vessel, none of us knowing how the currents ran on that coast. We all wondered why the skipper didn't anchor; but he said No, he must first show a light at the fore-topmast-head, and wait for an answering light on shore. We did wait, and nothing of the sort appeared. It was starlight and calm. What little wind there was came in puffs off the land. I suppose we waited, drifting a little to the westward, as I made it out, best part of an hour before anything happened—and then, instead of seeing the light on shore, we saw a boat coming toward us, rowed by two men only.

We hailed them, and they answered "Friends!" and hailed us by our name. They came on board. One of them was an Irishman, and the other was a coffee-colored native pilot, who jabbered a little English.

The Irishman handed a note to our skipper, who showed it to me. It informed us that the part of the coast we were off was not oversafe for discharging our cargo, seeing that spies of the enemy (that is to say, of the old Government) had been taken and shot in the neighborhood the day before. We might trust the brig to the native pilot; and he had his instructions to take us to another part of the coast. The note was signed by the proper parties; so we let the Irishman go back alone in the boat, and allowed the pilot to exercise his lawful authority over the brig. He kept us stretching off from the land till noon the next day—his instructions, seemingly, ordering him to keep up well out of sight of the shore. We only altered our course in the afternoon, so as to close in with the land again a little before midnight.

This same pilot was about as ill-looking a vagabond as ever I saw; a skinny, cowardly, quarrelsome mongrel, who swore at the men in the vilest broken English, till they were every one of them ready to pitch him overboard. The skipper kept them quiet, and I kept them quiet; for the pilot being given us by our instructions, we were bound to make the best of him. Near nightfall, however, with the best will in the world to avoid it, I was unlucky enough to quarrel with him.

He wanted to go below with his pipe, and I stopped him, of course, because it was contrary to orders. Upon that he tried to hustle by me, and I put him away with my hand. I never meant to push him down; but somehow I did. He picked himself up as quick as lightning, and pulled out his knife. I snatched it out of his hand, slapped his murderous face for him, and threw his weapon overboard. He gave me one ugly look, and walked aft. I didn't think much of the look then, but I remembered it a little too well afterward.

We were close in with the land again, just as the wind failed us, between eleven and twelve that night, and dropped anchor by the pilot's directions.

It was pitch-dark, and a dead airless calm. The skipper was on deck, with two of our best men for watch. The rest were below, except the pilot, who coiled himself up, more like a snake than a man, on the forecastle. It was not my watch till four in the morning. But I didn't like the look of the night, or the pilot, or the state of things generally, and I shook myself down on deck to get my nap there, and be ready for anything at a moment's notice. The last I remember was the skipper whispering to me that he didn't like the look of things either, and that he would go below and consult his instructions again. That is the last I remember, before the slow, heavy, regular roll of the old brig on the ground swell rocked me off to sleep.

I was awoke by a scuffle on the forecastle and a gag in my mouth. There was a man on my breast and a man on my legs, and I was bound hand and foot in half a minute.

The brig was in the hands of the Spaniards. They were swarming all over her. I heard six heavy splashes in the water, one after another. I saw the captain stabbed to the heart as he came running up the companion, and I heard a seventh splash in the water Except myself, every soul of us on board had been murdered and thrown into the sea. Why I was left I couldn't think, till I saw the pilot stoop over me with a lantern, and look, to make sure of who I was. There was a devilish grin on his face, and he nodded his head at me, as much as to say, *you* were the man who hustled me down and slapped my face, and I mean to play the game of cat and mouse with you in return for it!

I could neither move nor speak, but I could see the Spaniards take off the main hatch and rig the purchases for getting up the cargo. A quarter of an hour afterward I heard the sweeps of a schooner, or other small vessel, in the water. The strange craft was laid alongside of us, and the Spaniards set to work to discharge our cargo into her. They all worked hard except the pilot; and he came from time to time, with his lantern, to have another look at me, and to grin and nod, always in the same devilish way. I am old enough now not to be ashamed of confessing the truth, and I don't mind acknowledging that the pilot frightened me.

The fright, and the bonds, and the gag, and the not being able to stir hand or foot, had pretty nigh worn me out by the time the Spaniards gave over work. This was just as the dawn broke. They had shifted a good part of our cargo on board their vessel, but nothing like all of it, and they were sharp enough to be off with what they had got before daylight.

I need hardly say that I had made up my mind by this time to the worst I could think of. The pilot, it was clear enough, was one of the spies of the enemy, who had wormed himself into the confidence of our consignees without being suspected. He, or more likely his employers, had got knowledge enough of us to suspect what our cargo was; we had been anchored for the night in the safest berth for them to surprise us in; and we had paid the penalty of having a small crew, and consequently an insufficient watch. All this was clear enough—but what did the pilot mean to do with me?

On the word of a man, it makes my flesh creep now, only to tell you what he did with me.

After all the rest of them were out of the brig, except the pilot and two Spanish seamen, these last took me up, bound and gagged as I was, lowered me into the hold of the vessel, and laid me along the floor, lashing me to it with ropes' ends, so that I could just turn from one side to the other, but could not roll myself fairly over, so as to change my place. They then left me. Both of them were the worse for liquor; but the devil of a pilot was sober—mind that!—as sober as I am at the present moment.

I lay in the dark for a little while, with my heart thumping as if it was going to jump out of me. I lay about five minutes or so when the pilot came down into the hold alone.

He had the captain's cursed flat candlestick and a carpenter's awl in one hand, and a long thin twist of cotton yarn, well oiled, in the other. He put the candlestick, with a new "dip" candle lighted in it, down on the floor about two feet from my face, and close against the side of the vessel. The light was feeble enough; but it was sufficient to show a dozen barrels of gunpowder or more left all round me in the hold of the brig. I began to suspect what he was after the moment I noticed the barrels. The horrors laid hold of me from head to foot, and the sweat poured off my face like water.

I saw him go next to one of the barrels of powder standing against the side of the vessel in a line with the candle, and about three feet, or rather better, away from it. He bored a hole in the side of the barrel with his awl, and the horrid powder came trickling out, as black as hell, and dripped into the hollow of his hand, which he

held to catch it. When he had got a good handful, he stopped up the hole by jamming one end of his oiled twist of cotton yarn fast into it, and then he rubbed the powder into the whole length of the yarn till he had blackened every hair breadth of it.

The next thing he did—as true as I sit here, as true as the heaven above us all—the next thing he did was to carry the free end of his long, lean, black, frightful slow match to the lighted candle alongside my face. He tied it (the bloody-minded villain!) in several rows round the tallow dip, about a third of the distance down, measuring from the flame of the wick to the lip of the candlestick. He did that; he looked to see if the lashings were all safe; and then he put his face close to mine, and whispered in my ear, "Blow up with the brig!"

He was on deck again the moment after, and he and the two others shoved the hatch on over me. At the farthest end from where I lay they had not fitted it down quite true, and I saw a blink of daylight glimmering in when I looked in that direction. I heard the sweeps of the schooner fall into the water—splash! splash! fainter and fainter, as they swept the vessel out in the dead calm, to be ready for the wind in the offing. Fainter and fainter, splash, splash! for a quarter of an hour or more.

While those receding sounds were in my ears, my eyes were fixed on the candle.

It had been freshly lighted. If left to itself, it would burn for between six and seven hours. The slow match was twisted round it about a third of the way down, and therefore the flame would be about two hours reaching it. There I lay, gagged, bound, lashed to the floor; seeing my own life burning down with the candle by my side—there I lay, alone on the sea, doomed to be blown to atoms, and to see that doom drawing on, nearer and nearer with every fresh second of time, through nigh on two hours to come; powerless to help myself, and speechless to call for help to others. The wonder to me is that I didn't cheat the flame, the slow match, and the powder, and die of the horror of my situation before the first half hour was out in the hold of the brig.

I can't exactly say how long I kept command of my senses after I had ceased to hear the splash of the schooner's sweeps in the water. I can trace back everything I did and everything I thought up to a certain point; but, once past that, I get all abroad, and lose my-

73

AMERICAN WARSHIPS UNDER SAIL OFF THE SOUTH COAST OF ENGLAND

self in my memory now, much as I lost myself in my own feelings at the time.

The moment the hatch was covered over me, I began, as every other man would have begun in my place, with a frantic effort to free my hands. In the mad panic I was in, I cut my flesh with the lashings as if they had been knife blades, but I never stirred them. There was less chance still of freeing my legs, or of tearing myself from the fastenings that held me to the floor. I gave in when I was all but suffocated for want of breath. The gag, you will be pleased to remember, was a terrible enemy to me; I could only breathe freely through my nose—and that is but a poor vent when a man is straining his strength as far as ever it will go.

I gave in and lay quiet, and got my breath again, my eyes glaring and straining at the candle all the time. While I was staring at it, the notion struck me of trying to blow out the flame by pumping a long breath at it suddenly through my nostrils. It was too high above me, and too far away from me, to be reached in that fashion. I tried, and tried, and tried; and then I gave in again, and lay quiet again, always with my eyes glaring at the candle, and the candle glaring at me. The splash of the schooner's sweeps was very faint by this time. I could only just hear them in the morning stillness. Splash! splash!—fainter and fainter—splash! splash!

Without exactly feeling my mind going, I began to feel it getting queer as early as this. The snuff of the candle was growing taller and taller, and the length of tallow between the flame and the slow match, which was the length of my life, was getting shorter and shorter. I calculated that I had an hour and a half! Was there a chance in that time of a boat pulling off to the brig from shore? Whether the land near which the vessel was anchored was in possession of our side, or in possession of the enemy's side, I made out that they must, sooner or later, send to hail the brig merely because she was a stranger in those parts. The question for *me* was, how soon? The sun had not risen yet, as I could tell by looking through the chink in the hatch. There was no coast village near us, as we all knew, before the brig was seized, by seeing no lights on shore. There was no wind, as I could tell by listening, to bring any strange vessel near. If I had had six hours to live, there might have been a chance for me, reckoning from sunrise to noon. But with an hour and a half, which had dwindled to an hour and a quarter by this time—or in other words, with the earliness of the morning, the uninhabited coast, and the dead calm all against me—there was not the ghost of a chance. As I felt that, I had another struggle—the last—with my bonds, and only cut myself the deeper for my pains.

I gave in once more, and lay quiet, and listened for the splash of the sweeps.

Gone! Not a sound could I hear but the blowing of a fish now and then on the surface of the sea, and the creak of the old brig's crazy old spars, as she rolled gently from side to side with the little swell there was on the quiet water.

An hour and a quarter. The wick grew terribly as the quarter slipped away, and the charred top of it began to thicken and spread out mushroom-shape. It would fall off soon. Would it fall off red-hot, and would the swing of the brig cant it over the side of the candle and let it down on the slow match? If it would, I had about ten minutes to live instead of an hour.

This discovery set my mind for a minute on a new tack altogether. I began to ponder with myself what sort of death blowing up might be. Painful! Well, it would be, surely, too sudden for that. Perhaps just one crash inside me, or outside, or both; and nothing more! Perhaps not even a crash; that and death and the scattering of this living body of mine into millions of fiery sparks, might all happen in the same instant! I couldn't make it out; I couldn't settle how it would be. The minute of calmness in my mind left it before I had half done thinking; and I got all abroad again.

When I came back to my thoughts, or when they came back to me (I can't say which), the wick was awfully tall, the flame was burning with a smoke above it, the charred top was broad and red, and heavily spreading out to its fall.

My despair and horror at seeing it took me in a new way, which was good and right, at any rate, for my poor soul. I tried to pray—in my own heart, you will understand, for the gag put all lip-praying out of my power. I tried, but the candle seemed to burn it up in me. I struggled hard to force my eyes from the slow, murdering flame, and to look up through the chink in the hatch at the blessed daylight. I tried once, tried twice; and gave it up. I next tried only to shut my eyes, and keep them shut—once—twice—and the second time I did it.

"God bless old mother, and sister Lizzie; God keep them both, and forgive *me.*" That was all I had time to say in my own heart, before my eyes opened again, in spite of me, and the flame of the candle flew into them, flew all over me, and burned up the rest of my thoughts in an instant.

I couldn't hear the fish blowing now; I couldn't hear the creak of the spars; I couldn't think; I couldn't feel the sweat of my own death agony on my face—I could only look at the heavy, charred top of the wick. It swelled, tottered, bent over to one side, dropped—red-hot at the moment of its fall—black and harmless, even before the swing of the brig had canted it over into the bottom of the candlestick.

I caught myself laughing.

Yes! laughing at the safe fall of the bit of wick. But for the gag, I should have screamed with laughter. As it was, I shook with it inside me—shook till the blood was in my head, and I was all but suffocated for want of breath. I had just sense enough left to feel that my own horrid laughter at that awful moment was a sign of my brain going at last. I had just sense enough to make another struggle before my mind broke loose like a frightened horse, and ran away with me.

One comforting look at the blink of daylight through the hatch was what I tried for once more. The fight to force my eyes from the candle and to get that one look at the daylight was the hardest I had yet; and I lost the fight. The flame had hold of my eyes as fast as the lashings had hold of my hands. I couldn't look away from it. I couldn't even shut my eyes, when I tried that next for the second time. There was the wick growing tall once more. There was the space of unburned candle between the light and the slow match shortened to an inch or less.

How much life did that inch leave me? Three quarters of an hour? Half an hour? Fifty minutes? Twenty minutes? Steady! an inch of tallow candle would burn longer than twenty minutes. An inch of tallow! the notion of a man's body and soul being kept together by an inch of tallow! Wonderful! Why the greatest king that sits on a throne can't keep a man's body and soul together; and here's an inch of tallow that can do what the king can't! There's something to tell my mother when I get home which will surprise her more than all the rest of my voyages put together. I laughed inwardly again at the thought of that, and shook and swelled and suffocated myself, till the light of the candle leaped in through my eyes, and licked up the laughter, and burned it out of me, and made me all empty and cold and quiet once more.

Mother and Lizzie. I don't know when they came back; but they did come back—not, as it seemed to me, into my mind this time, but right down bodily before me, in the hold of the brig.

Yes, sure enough, there was Lizzie, just as light-hearted as usual, laughing at me. Laughing? Well, why not? Who is to blame Lizzie for thinking I'm lying on my back, drunk in the cellar, with the beer barrels all round me? Steady! she's crying now—spinning round and round in a fiery mist, wringing her hands, screeching out for help—fainter and fainter, like the splash of the schooner's sweeps. Gone—burned up in the fiery mist! Mist? fire? no; neither one nor the other. It's mother makes the light—mother knitting, with ten flaming points at the ends of her fingers and thumbs, and slow matches hanging in bunches all round her face instead of her own grey hair. Mother in her old arm-chair, and the pilot's long skinny hands hanging over the back of the chair, dripping with gunpowder. No! no gunpowder, no chair, no mother—nothing but the pilot's face, shining red-hot, like a sun, in the fiery mist; turning upside down in the fiery mist; running backward and forward along the slow match, in the fiery mist; spinning millions of miles in a minute, in the fiery mist—spinning itself smaller and smaller into one tiny point, and that point darting on a sudden straight into my head—and then, all fire and all mist—no hearing, no seeing, no thinking, no feeling—the brig, the sea, my own self; the whole world, all gone together!

After what I've just told you, I know nothing and remember nothing till I woke up (as it seemed to me) in a comfortable bed, with two rough-and-ready men like myself sitting on each side of my pillow, and a gentleman standing watching me at the foot of the bed. It was about seven in the morning. My sleep (or what seemed like my sleep to me) had lasted better than eight months—I was among my own countrymen in the island of Trinidad—the men at each side of my pillow were my keepers, turn and turn about—and the gentleman standing at the foot oft the bed was the doctor. What I said and did in those eight months I never have

known, and never shall. I woke out of it as if it had been one long sleep—that's all I know.

It was another two months or more before the doctor thought it safe to answer the questions I asked him.

An American vessel, becalmed in the offing, had made out the brig as the sun rose; and the captain, seeing her anchored where no vessel had any reason to be, had manned one of his boats and sent his mate to look into the matter and report of what he saw.

What he saw, when he and his men found the brig deserted and boarded her, was a gleam of candlelight through the chink in the hatchway. The flame was within about a thread's breadth of the slow match when he lowered himself into the hold; and if he had not had the sense and coolness to cut the match in two with his knife before he touched the candle, he and his men might have been blown up along with the brig as well as me. The match caught, and turned into sputtering red fire, in the very act of putting the candle out.

What became of the Spanish schooner and the pilot I have never heard.

As for the brig, the Yankees took her, as they took me, to Trinidad, and claimed their salvage, and got it, I hope, for their own sakes. I was landed just in the same state as when they rescued me from the brig—that is to say, clean out of my senses. But please to remember, it was a long time ago; and, take my word for it, I was discharged cured, as I have told you. Bless your hearts. I'm all right now, as you may see. I'm a little shaken by telling the story, as is only natural—a little shaken, my good friends, that's all.

As a young man, Wilkie Collins (1824–1889) was apprenticed to a successful tea merchant, but gave up a business career to be a writer of detective novels. This bone-chilling tale was first published in 1859.

The Treacherous Sea

Rounding Cape Horn

Herman Melville

And now, through drizzling fogs and vapors, and under damp, double-reefed topsails, our wet-decked frigate drew nearer and nearer to the squally Cape.

Who has not heard of it? Cape Horn, Cape Horn—a *horn* indeed, that has tossed many a good ship. Was the descent of Orpheus, Ulysses, or Dante into Hell, one whit more hardy and sublime than the first navigator's weathering of that terrible Cape?

Turned on her heel by a fierce west wind, many an outward-bound ship has been driven across the Southern Ocean to the Cape of Good Hope—that way to seek a passage to the Pacific. And that stormy Cape, I doubt not, has sent many a fine craft to the bottom, and told no tales. At those ends of the earth are no chronicles. What signify the broken spars and shrouds that, day after day, are driven before the prows of more fortunate vessels? or the tall masts, imbedded in icebergs, that are found floating by? They but hint the old story—of ships that have sailed from their ports, and never more have been heard of.

Impracticable Cape! You may approach it from this direction or that—in any way you please—from the East or from the West; with the wind astern, or abeam, or on the quarter; and still Cape Horn is Cape Horn. Cape Horn it is that takes the conceit out of freshwater sailors, and steeps in a still salter brine the saltest. Woe betide the tyro; the foolhardy, Heaven preserve!

Your Mediterranean captain, who with a cargo of oranges has hitherto made merry runs across the Atlantic, without so much as furling a t'gallant sail, oftentimes, off Cape Horn, receives a lesson which he carries to the grave; though the grave—as is too often the case—follows so hard on the lesson that no benefit comes from the experience.

Other strangers who draw nigh to this Patagonia termination of our Continent, with their souls full of its shipwrecks and disasters—topsails cautiously reefed, and everything guardedly snug—these strangers at first unexpectedly encountering a tolerably smooth sea, rashly conclude that the Cape, after all, is but a bugbear; they have been imposed upon by fables, and founderings and sinkings hereabouts are all cock-and-bull stories.

"Out reefs, my hearties; fore and aft set t'gallant sails! stand by to give her the fore-topmast stun' sail!"

But, Captain Rash, those sails of yours were much safer in the sail maker's loft. For now, while the heedless craft is bounding over the billows, a black cloud rises out of the sea; the sun drops down from the sky; a horrible mist far and wide spreads over the water.

"Hands by the halyards! Let go! Clew up!"

Too late. For ere the ropes' ends can be cast off from the pins, the tornado is blowing down to the bottom of their throats. The masts are willows, the sails ribbons, the cordage wool; the whole ship is brewed into the yeast of the gale.

And now, if, when the first green sea breaks over him, Captain Rash is not swept overboard, he has his hands full be sure. In all probability his three masts have gone by the board, and, raveled into list, his sails are floating in the air. Or, perhaps, the ship *broaches to*, or is *brought by the lee*. In either case, Heaven help the sailors, their wives and their little ones; and Heaven help the underwriters.

Familiarity with danger makes a brave man braver, but less daring. Thus with seamen: he who goes the oftenest round Cape Horn goes the most circumspectly. A veteran mariner is never deceived by the treacherous breezes which sometimes waft him pleasantly toward the latitude of the Cape. No sooner does he come within a certain distance of it—previously fixed in his own mind—than all hands are turned to setting the ship in storm trim; and never mind how light the breeze, down come his t'gallant yards. He "bends" his strongest storm sails, and lashes everything on deck securely. The ship is then ready for the worst; and if, in reeling round the headland, she receives a broadside, it generally goes well with her. If ill, all hands go to the bottom with quiet consciences.

Among sea captains, there are some who seem to regard the genius of the Cape as a wilful, capricious jade, that must be courted and coaxed into complaisance. First, they come along under easy sails; do not steer boldly for the headland, but tack this way and that—sidling up to it. Now they woo the Jezebel with a t'gallant studding sail; anon, they deprecate her wrath with double-reefed topsails. When, at length, her unappeasable fury is fairly aroused, and all round the dismantled ship the storm howls and howls for days together, they still persevere in their efforts. First, they try unconditional submission; furling every rag and *heaving to*; laying like a log, for the tempest to toss wheresoever it pleases.

This failing, they set a *spencer* or *trysail*, and shift on the other tack. Equally vain! The gale sings as hoarsely as before. At last, the wind comes round fair; they drop the foresail; square the yards, and scud before it; their implacable foe chasing them with tornadoes, as if to show her insensibility to the last.

Other ships, without encountering these terrible gales, spend week after week endeavoring to turn this boisterous world-corner against a continual head wind. Tacking hither and thither, in the language of sailors they *polish* the Cape by beating about its edges so long.

Le Mair and Schouten, two Dutchmen, were the first navigators who weathered Cape Horn. Previous to this, passages had been made to the Pacific by the Straits of Magellan; nor, indeed, at that period, was it known to a certainty that there was any other route, or that the land now called Terra del Fuego was an island. A few leagues southward from Terra del Fuego is a cluster of small islands, the Diegoes; between which and the former island are the Straits of Le Mair, so called in honor of their discoverer, who first sailed through them into the Pacific. Le Mair and Schouten, in their small, clumsy vessels, encountered a series of tremendous gales, the prelude to the long train of similar hardships which most of their followers have experienced. It is a significant fact, that Schouten's vessel, the *Horne*, which gave its name to the Cape, was almost lost in weathering it.

The next navigator round the Cape was Sir Francis Drake, who, on Raleigh's Expedition, beholding for the first time, from the Isthmus of Darien, the "goodlie South Sea," like a true-born Englishman, vowed, please God, to sail an English ship thereon; which the gallant sailor did, to the sore discomfiture of the Spaniards on the coasts of Chile and Peru.

But perhaps the greatest hardships on record, in making this celebrated passage, were those experienced by Lord Anson's squadron in 1736. Three remarkable and most interesting narratives record their disasters and sufferings. The first, jointly written by the carpenter and gunner of the *Wager*; the second, by young Byron, a midshipman in the same ship; the third, by the chaplain of the *Centurion*. *White Jacket* has them all; and they are fine reading of a boisterous March night, with the casement rattling in your ear, and the chimney-stacks blowing down upon the pavement, bubbling with raindrops.

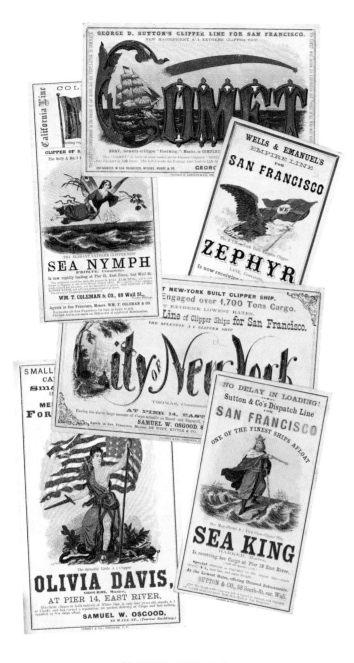

CLIPPER SHIP CARDS

But if you want the best idea of Cape Horn, get my friend Dana's unmatchable *Two Years Before the Mast.* But you can read, and so you must have read it. His chapters describing Cape Horn must have been written with an icicle.

At the present day the horrors of the Cape have somewhat abated. This is owing to a growing familiarity with it; but, more than all, to the improved condition of ships in all respects, and the means now generally in use of preserving the health of the crews in times of severe and prolonged exposure.

Colder and colder; we are drawing nigh to the Cape. Now gregoes, pea jackets, monkey jackets, reefing jackets, storm jackets, oil jackets, paint jackets, round jackets, short jackets, long jackets, and all manner of jackets, are the order of the day, not excepting the immortal white jacket, which begins to be sturdily buttoned up to the throat, and pulled down vigorously at the skirts, to bring them well over the loins.

But, alas! those skirts were lamentably scanty; and though, with its quiltings, the jacket was stuffed out about the breasts like a Christmas turkey, and of a dry cold day kept the wearer warm enough in that vicinity, yet about the loins it was shorter than a ballet dancer's skirts; so that while my chest was in the temperate zone close adjoining the torrid, my hapless thighs were in Nova Zembla, hardly an icicle's toss from the Pole.

Then, again, the repeated soakings and dryings it had undergone had by this time made it shrink woefully all over, especially in the arms, so that the wristbands had gradually crawled up near to the elbows; and it required an energetic thrust to push the arm through, in drawing the jacket on.

I endeavored to amend these misfortunes by sewing a sort of canvas ruffle round the skirts, by way of a continuation or supplement to the original work, and by doing the same with the wristbands.

This is the time for oilskin suits, dreadnoughts, tarred trousers and overalls, seaboots, comforters, mittens woolen socks, Guernsey frocks, Havre shirts, buffalo-robe shirts, and moose-skin drawers. Every man's jacket is his wigwam, and every man's hat his caboose.

Perfect license is now permitted to the men respecting their clothing. Whatever they can rake and scrape together they put on—swaddling themselves in old sails, and drawing old socks over their heads for nightcaps. This is the time for smiting your chest with your hand, and talking loud to keep up the circulation.

Colder, and colder, and colder, till at last we spoke a fleet of icebergs bound North. After that, it was one incessant "cold snap," that almost snapped off our fingers and toes. Cold! It was cold as *Blue Flujin*, where sailors say fire freezes.

And now coming up with the latitude of the Cape, we stood southward to give it a wide berth, and while so doing were becalmed; ay, becalmed off Cape Horn, which is worse, far worse, than being becalmed on the Line.

Here we lay forty-eight hours, during which the cold was intense. I wondered at the liquid sea, which refused to freeze in such a temperature. The clear, cold sky overhead looked like a steel-blue cymbal, that might ring, could you smite it. Our breath came and went like puffs of smoke from pipe bowls. At first there was a long gauky swell, that obliged us to furl most of the sails, and even send down t'gallant yards, for fear of pitching them overboard.

Out of sight of land, at this extremity of both the inhabitable and uninhabitable world, our peopled frigate, echoing with the voices of men, the bleating of lambs, the cackling of fowls, the gruntings of pigs, seemed like Noah's old ark itself, becalmed at the climax of the Deluge.

There was nothing to be done but patiently to await the pleasure of the elements, and "whistle for a wind," the usual practice of seamen in a calm. No fire was allowed, except for the indispensable purpose of cooking, and heating bottles of water to toast Selvagee's feet. He who possessed the largest stock of vitality, stood the best chance to escape freezing. It was horrifying. In such weather any man could have undergone amputation with great ease, and helped take up the arteries himself.

Indeed, this state of affairs had not lasted quite twenty-four hours, when the extreme frigidity of the air, united to our increased tendency to inactivity, would very soon have rendered some of us subjects for the surgeon and his mates, had not a humane proceeding of the captain suddenly impelled us to rigorous exercise.

And here be it said, that the appearance of the boatswain, with his silver whistle to his mouth, at the main hatchway of the gun deck, is always regarded by the crew with the utmost curiosity, for this betokens that some general order is about to be promulgated through the ship. What now? is the question that runs on from man to man. A short preliminary whistle is then given by "Old Yarn," as they call him, which whistle serves to collect round him, from their various stations, his four mates. Then Yarn, or Pipes, as leader of the orchestra, begins a peculiar call, in which his assistants join. This over, the order, whatever it may be, is loudly sung out and prolonged, till the remotest corner echoes again. The boatswain and his mates are the town criers of a man-of-war.

The calm had commenced in the afternoon: and the following morning the ship's company were electrified by a general order, thus set forth and declared: *"D'ye hear there, fore and aft! all hands skylark!"*

This mandate, nowadays never used except upon very rare occasions, produced the same effect upon the men that Exhilarating Gas would have done, or an extra allowance of "grog." For a time, the wonted discipline of the ship was broken through, and perfect license allowed. It was a Babel here, a Bedlam there, and a Pandemonium everywhere. The Theatricals were nothing compared with it. Then the fainthearted and timorous crawled to their hiding places, and the lusty and bold shouted forth their glee. Gangs of men, in all sorts of outlandish habiliments, wild as those worn at some crazy carnival, rushed to and fro, seizing upon whomsoever they pleased—warrant officers and dangerous pugilists excepted—pulling and hauling the luckless tars about, till fairly baited into a genial warmth. Some were made fast to and hoisted aloft with a will: others, mounted upon oars, were ridden fore and aft on a rail, to the boisterous mirth of the spectators, any one of whom might be the next victim. Swings were rigged from the tops, or the masts; and the most reluctant wights being purposely selected, spite of all struggles, were swung from east to west, in vast arcs of circles, till almost breathless. Hornpipes, fandangoes, Donnybrook-jigs, reels, and quadrilles, were danced under the very nose of the most mighty captain, and upon the very quarter-deck and poop. Sparring and wrestling, too, were all the vogue; *Kentucky bites* were given, and the *Indian hug* exchanged. The din frightened the seafowl that flew by with accelerated wing.

It is worth mentioning that several casualties occurred, of which, however, I will relate but one. While the "skylarking" was at its height, one of the foretopmen—an ugly-tempered devil of a Portuguese, looking on—swore that he would be the death of any man who laid violent hands upon his inviolable person. This threat being overheard, a band of desperadoes, coming up from behind, tripped him up in an instant, and in the twinkling of an eye the Portuguese was straddling an oar, borne aloft by an uproarious multitude who rushed him along the deck at a railroad gallop. The living mass of arms all round and beneath him was so dense, that every time he inclined to one side he was instantly pushed upright, but only to fall over again, to receive another push from the contrary direction. Presently, disengaging his hands from those who held them, the enraged seaman drew from his bosom an iron belaying pin, and recklessly laid about him to right and left. Most of his persecutors fled; but some eight or ten still stood their ground, and, while bearing him aloft, endeavored to wrest the weapon from his hands. In this attempt, one man was struck on the head, and dropped insensible. He was taken up for dead, and carried below to Cuticle, the surgeon, while the Portuguese was put under guard. But the wound did not prove very serious; and in a few days the man was walking about the deck, with his head well bandaged.

This occurrence put an end to the "skylarking," further head-breaking being strictly prohibited. In due time the Portuguese paid the penalty of his rashness at the gangway; while once again the officers *shipped their quarterdeck faces.*

Ere the calm had yet left us, a sail had been discerned from the fore-topmasthead, at a great distance, probably three leagues or more. At first it was a mere speck, altogether out of sight from the deck. By the force of attraction, or something else equally inscrutable, two ships in a calm, and equally affected by the currents, will always approximate, more or less. Though there was not a breath of wind, it was not a great while before the strange sail was described from our bulwarks; gradually, it drew still nearer.

What was she, and whence? There is no object which so excites interest and conjecture, and, at the same time, baffles both, as a sail, seen as a mere speck on these remote seas off Cape Horn.

A breeze! a breeze! for lo! the stranger is now perceptibly nearing the frigate; the officer's spyglass pronounces her a full-rigged ship, with all sail set and coming right down to us, though in our own vicinity the calm still reigns.

She is bringing the wind with her. Hurrah! Ay, there it is! Behold how mincingly it creeps over the sea, just ruffling and crisping it.

Our topmen were at once sent aloft to loose the sails, and presently they faintly began to distend. As yet we hardly had steerageway. Toward sunset the stranger bore down before the wind, a complete pyramid of canvas. Never before, I venture to say, was Cape Horn so audaciously insulted. Stun' sails alow and aloft; royals, moon sails, and everything else. She glided under our stern, within hailing distance, and the signal quartermaster ran up our ensign to the gaff.

"Ship ahoy!" cried the lieutenant of the watch, through his trumpet.

"Halloa!" bawled an old fellow in a green jacket, clapping one hand to his mouth, while he held on with the other to the mizzen-shrouds.

"What ship's that?"

"The *Sultan,* Indiaman, from New York, and bound to Callao and Canton, sixty days out, all well. What frigate's that?"

"The United States ship *Neversink,* homeward bound."

"Hurrah! hurrah! hurrah!" yelled our enthusiastic countryman, transported with patriotism.

By this time the *Sultan* had swept past, but the lieutenant of the watch could not withhold a parting admonition.

"D'ye hear? You'd better take in some of your flying-kites there. Look out for Cape Horn!"

But the friendly advice was lost in the now increasing wind. With a suddenness by no means unusual in these latitudes, the light breeze soon became a succession of sharp squalls, and our sail-proud braggadacio of an *Indiaman* was observed to let everything go by the run, his t'gallant stun' sails and flying-jib taking quick leave of the spars; the flying-jib was swept into the air, rolled together for a few minutes, and tossed about in the squalls like a football. But the wind played no such pranks with the more prudently managed canvas of the *Neversink,* though before many hours it was stirring times with us.

CLIPPER SHIP CARD FOR THE I.F. CHAPMAN

About midnight, when the starboard watch, to which, I belonged, was below, the boatswain's whistle was heard, followed by the shrill cry of "All hands take in sail! jump, men, and save ship!"

Springing from our hammocks, we found the frigate leaning over to it so steeply, that it was with difficulty we could climb the ladders leading to the upper deck.

Here the scene was awful. The vessel seemed to be sailing on her side. The main-deck guns had several days previous been run in and housed, and the portholes closed, but the lee carronades on the quarterdeck and forecastle were plunging through the sea, which undulated over them in milk-like billows of foam. With every lurch to leeward the yardarm-ends seemed to dip in the sea, while forward the spray dashed over the bows in cataracts, and drenched the men who were on the foreyard. By this time the deck was alive with the whole strength of the ship's company, five hundred men, officers and all, mostly clinging to the weather bulwarks. The occasional phosphorescence of the yeasting sea cast a glare upon their uplifted faces, as a night fire in a populous city lights up the panic-stricken crowd.

In a sudden gale, or when a large quantity of sail is suddenly to be furled, it is the custom for the first lieutenant to take the trumpet from whoever happens then to be officer of the deck. But Mad Jack had the trumpet that watch; nor did the first lieutenant now seek to wrest it from his hands. Every eye was upon him, as if we had chosen him from among us all, to decide this battle with the elements, by single combat with the spirit of the Cape; for Mad Jack was the saving genius of the ship, and so proved himself that night. I owe this right hand, that is this moment flying over my sheet, and all my present being to Mad Jack. The ship's bows were now butting, battering, ramming, and thundering over and upon the head seas, and with a horrible wallowing sound our whole hull was rolling in the trough of the foam. The gale came athwart the deck, and every sail seemed bursting with its wild breath.

All the quartermasters, and several of the forecastle-men, were swarming round the double-wheel on the quarterdeck. Some jumping up and down, with their hands upon the spokes; for the whole helm and galvanized keel were fiercely feverish, with the life imparted to them by the wild tempest.

"Hard up the helm!" shouted Captain Claret, bursting from his cabin like a ghost in his nightdress.

"Damn you!" raged Mad Jack to the quartermasters; "hard *down*—hard *down*, I say, and be damned to you!"

Contrary orders! but Mad Jack's were obeyed. His object was to throw the ship into the wind, so as the better to admit of close-reefing the topsails. But though the halyards were let go, it was impossible to clew down the yards, owing to the enormous horizontal strain on the canvas. It now blew a hurricane. The spray flew over the ship in floods. The gigantic masts seemed about to snap under the world-wide strain of the three entire topsails.

"Clew down! clew down!" shouted Mad Jack, husky with excitement, and in a frenzy, beating his trumpet against one of the shrouds. But, owing to the slant of the ship, the thing could not be done. It was obvious that before many minutes something must go—either sails, rigging, or sticks; perhaps the hull itself, and all hands.

Presently a voice from the top exclaimed that there was a rent in the main-topsail. And instantly we heard a report like two or three muskets discharged together; the vast sail was rent up and down like the Veil of the Temple. This saved the mainmast; for the yard was now clewed down with comparative ease, and the topmen laid out to stow the shattered canvas. Soon the two remaining topsails were also clewed down and close reefed.

Above all the roar of the tempest and the shouts of the crew, was heard the dismal tolling of the ship's bell—almost as large as that of a village church—which the violent rolling of the ship was occasioning. Imagina-

tion cannot conceive the horror of such a sound in a night-tempest at sea.

"Stop that ghost!" roared Mad Jack; "away, one of you, and wrench off the clapper!"

But no sooner was this ghost gagged, than a still more appalling sound was heard, the rolling to and fro of the heavy shot, which, on the gun deck, had broken loose from the gun racks, and converted that part of the ship into an immense bowling alley. Some hands were sent down to secure them; but it was as much as their lives were worth. Several were maimed; and the midshipmen who were ordered to see the duty performed reported it impossible, until the storm abated.

The most terrific job of all was to furl the mainsail, which, at the commencement of the squalls, had been clewed up, coaxed and quieted as much as possible with the bunt-lines and slab-lines. Mad Jack waited some time for a lull, ere he gave an order so perilous to be executed. For to furl this enormous sail, in such a gale, required at least fifty men on the yard; whose weight, superadded to that of the ponderous stick itself, still further jeopardized their lives. But there was no prospect of a cessation of the gale, and the order was at last given.

At this time a hurricane of slanting sleet and hail was descending upon us; the rigging was coated with a thin glare of ice, formed within the hour.

"Aloft, mainyard men! and all you main-top men! and furl the mainsail!" cried Mad Jack.

I dashed down my hat, slipped out of my quilted jacket in an instant, kicked the shoes from my feet, and, with a crowd of others, sprang for the rigging. Above the bulwarks (which in a frigate are so high as to afford much protection to those on deck) the gale was horrible. The sheer force of the wind flattened us to the rigging as we ascended, and every hand seemed congealing to the icy shrouds by which we held.

"Up—up, my brave hearties!" shouted Mad Jack; and up we got, some way or other, all of us, and groped our way out on the yardarms.

"Hold on, every mother's son!" cried an old quarter-gunner at my side. He was bawling at the top of his compass; but in the gale, he seemed to be whispering; and I only heard him from his being right to windward of me.

But his hint was unnecessary; I dug my nails into the *Jack-stays*, and swore that nothing but death should part me and them until I was able to turn round and look to windward. As yet, this was impossible; I could scarcely hear the man to leeward at my elbow; the wind seemed to snatch the words from his mouth and fly away with them to the South Pole.

All this while the sail itself was flying about, sometimes catching over our heads, and threatening to tear us from the yard in spite of all our hugging. For about three quarters of an hour we thus hung suspended right over the rampant billows, which curled their very crests under the feet of some four or five of us clinging to the lee-yardarm, as if to float us from our place.

Presently, the word passed along the yard from windward, that we were ordered to come down and leave the sail to blow, since it could not be furled. A midshipman, it seemed, had been sent up by the officer of the deck to give the order, as no trumpet could be heard where we were.

Those on the weather yardarm managed to crawl upon the spar and scramble down the rigging; but with us, upon the extreme leeward side, this feat was out of the question; it was, literary, like climbing a precipice to get to windward in order to reach the shrouds: besides, the entire yard was now encased in ice, and our hands and feet were so numb that we dared not trust our lives to them. Nevertheless, by assisting each other, we contrived to throw ourselves prostrate along the yard, and embrace it with our arms and legs. In this position, the stun' sail booms greatly assisted in securing our hold. Strange as it may appear, I do not suppose that, at this moment, the slightest sensation of fear was felt by one man on that yard. We clung to it with might and main; but this was instinct. The truth is, that, in circumstances like these, the sense of fear is annihilated in the unutterable sights that fill all the eye, and the sounds that fill all the ear. You become identified with the tempest; your insignificance is lost in the riot of the stormy universe around.

Below us, our noble frigate seemed thrice its real length—a vast black wedge, opposing its widest end to the combined fury of the sea and wind.

At length the first fury of the gale began to abate, and we at once fell to pounding our hands, as a preliminary operation to going to work; for a gang of men had now ascended to help secure what was left of the sail; we somehow packed it away, at last, and came down.

About noon the next day, the gale so moderated that we shook two reefs out of the topsails, set new courses, and stood due east, with the wind astern. Thus, all the fine weather we encountered after first weighing anchor on the pleasant Spanish coast, was but the prelude to this one terrific night; more especially, that treacherous calm immediately preceding it. But how could we reach our long-promised homes without encountering Cape Horn? by what possibility avoid it? And though some ships have weathered it without these perils, yet by far the greater part must encounter them. Lucky it is that it comes about midway in the homeward-bound passage, so that the sailors have time to prepare for it, and time to recover from it after it is astern.

But, sailor or landsman, there is some sort of a Cape Horn for all. Boys! beware of it; prepare for it in time. Graybeards! thank God it is passed. And ye lucky livers, to whom, by some rare fatality, your Cape Horns are placid as Lake Lemans, flatter not yourselves that good luck is judgment and discretion; for all the yolk in your eggs, you might have foundered and gone down, had the spirit of the Cape said the word.

This story is from the novel White-Jacket *(1850).*

Make Westing

Jack London

Whatever you do, make westing! make westing!
—Sailing directions for Cape Horn.

For seven weeks the *Mary Rogers* had been between 50° south in the Atlantic and 50° south in the Pacific, which meant that for seven weeks she had been struggling to round Cape Horn. For seven weeks she had been either in dirt, or close to dirt, save once, and then, following upon six days of excessive dirt, which she had ridden out under the shelter of the redoubtable Tierra Del Fuego coast, she had almost gone ashore during a heavy swell in the dead calm that had suddenly fallen. For seven weeks she had wrestled with the Cape Horn graybeards, and in return been buffeted and smashed by them. She was a wooden ship, and her ceaseless straining had opened her seams, so that twice a day the watch took its turn at the pumps.

The *Mary Rogers* was strained, the crew was strained, and big Dan Cullen, master, was likewise strained. Perhaps he was strained most of all, for upon him rested the responsibility of that titanic struggle. He slept most of the time in his clothes, though he rarely slept. He haunted the deck at night, a great, burly, robust ghost, black with the sunburn of thirty years of sea and hairy as an orangutan. He, in turn, was haunted by one thought of action, a sailing direction for the Horn: *Whatever you do, make westing! make westing!* It was an obsession. He thought of nothing else, except, at times, to blaspheme God for sending such bitter weather.

Make westing! He hugged the Horn, and a dozen times lay hove to with the iron Cape bearing east-by-north, or north-north-east, a score of miles away. And each time the eternal west wind smote him back and he made easting. He fought gale after gale, south to 64°, inside the antarctic drift-ice, and pledged his immortal soul to the Powers of Darkness for a bit of westing, for a slant to take him around. And he made easting. In despair, he had tried to make the passage through the Straits of Le Maire. Halfway through, the wind hauled to the north'ard of northwest, the glass dropped to 28.88, and he turned and ran before a gale of cyclonic fury, missing, by a hair's breadth, piling up the *Mary Rogers* on the black-toothed rocks. Twice he had made west to the Diego Ramirez Rocks, one of the times saved between two snow-squalls by sighting the gravestones of ships a quarter of a mile dead ahead.

Blow! Captain Dan Cullen instanced all his thirty years at sea to prove that never had it blown so before. The *Mary Rogers* was hove to at the time he gave the evidence, and, to clinch it, inside half an hour the *Mary Rogers* was hove down to the hatches. Her new main-topsail and brand new spencer were blown away like tissue paper; and five sails, furled and fast under double gaskets, were blown loose and stripped from the yards. And before morning the *Mary Rogers* was hove down twice again, and holes were knocked in her bulwarks to ease her decks from the weight of ocean that pressed her down.

On an average of once a week Captain Dan Cullen caught glimpses of the sun. Once, for ten minutes, the sun shone at midday, and ten minutes afterward a new gale was piping up, both watches were shortening sail and all was buried in the obscurity of a driving snow-squall. For a fortnight once, Captain Dan Cullen was without a meridian or a chronometer sight. Rarely did he know his position within half a degree, except when in sight of land; for sun and stars remained hidden behind the sky, and it was so gloomy that even at the best the horizons were poor for accurate observations. A gray gloom shrouded the world. The clouds were gray; the great driving seas were leaden gray; the smoking crests were a gray churning; even the occasional albatrosses were gray, while the snow flurries were not white, but gray, under the sombre pall of the heavens.

Life on board the *Mary Rogers* was gray—gray and gloomy. The faces of the sailors were blue-gray; they were afflicted with sea-cuts and sea-boils, and suffered exquisitely. They were shadows of men. For seven weeks, in the forecastle or on deck, they had not known what it was to be dry. They had forgotten what it was to sleep out a watch, and all watches it was, "All hands on deck!" They caught snatches of agonized sleep, and they slept in their oilskins ready for the everlasting call. So weak and worn were they that it took both watches to do the work of one. That was why both watches were on deck so much of the time. And no shadow of a man could shirk duty. Nothing less than a broken leg could enable a man to knock off work; and there were two such, who had been mauled and pulped by the seas that broke aboard.

One other man who was the shadow of a man was George Dorety. He was the only passenger on board, a friend of the firm, and he had elected to make the voyage for his health. But seven weeks of Cape Horn had not bettered his health. He gasped and panted in his bunk through the long heaving nights; and when on deck he was so bundled up for warmth that he resembled a peripatetic old-clothes shop. At midday, eating at the cabin table in a gloom so deep that the swinging sea-lamps burned always, he looked as blue-gray as the sickest, saddest man for'ard. Nor did gazing across the table at Captain Dan Cullen have any cheering effect upon him. Captain Cullen chewed and scowled and kept silent. The scowls were for God, and with every chew he reiterated the sole thought of his existence, which was *make westing*. He was a big, hairy brute, and the sight of him was not stimulating to the other's appetite. He looked upon George Dorety as a Jonah, and told him so, once each meal, savagely transferring the scowl from God to the passenger and back again.

Nor did the mate prove a first aid to a languid appetite. Joshua Higgins by name, a seaman by profession and pull, but a potwalloper by capacity, he was a loose-jointed, sniffling creature, heartless and selfish and cowardly, without a soul, in fear of his life of Dan Cullen, and a bully over the sailors, who knew that behind the mate was Captain Cullen, the lawgiver and compeller, the driver and the destroyer, the incarnation of a dozen bucko mates. In that wild weather at the southern end of the earth, Joshua Higgins ceased washing. His grimy face usually robbed George Dorety of what little appetite he managed to accumulate. Ordinarily this lavatorial dereliction would have caught Captain Cullen's eye and vocabulary, but in the present his mind was filled with making westing, to the exclusion of all other things not contributory thereto. Whether the mate's face was clean or dirty had no bearing upon westing. Later on, when 50° south in the Pacific had been reached, Joshua Higgins would wash his face very abruptly. In the meantime, at the cabin table, where gray twilight alternated with lamplight while the lamps were being filled, George Dorety sat between the two men, one a tiger and the other a hyena, and wondered why God had made them. The second mate, Matthew Turner, was a true sailor and a man, but George Dorety did not have the solace of his company, for he ate by himself, solitary, when they had finished.

On Saturday morning, July 24, George Dorety awoke to a feeling of life and headlong movement. On deck he found the *Mary Rogers* running off before a

PORTRAIT OF A PACKET SHIP CAPTAIN

howling southeaster. Nothing was set but the lower topsails and the foresail. It was all she could stand, yet she was making fourteen knots, as Mr. Turner shouted in Dorety's ear when he came on deck. And it was all westing. She was going around the Horn at last . . . if the wind held. Mr. Turner looked happy. The end of the struggle was in sight. But Captain Cullen did not look happy. He scowled at Dorety in passing. Captain Cullen did not want God to know that he was pleased with that wind. He had a conception of a malicious God, and believed in his secret soul that if God knew it was a desirable wind, God would promptly efface it and send a snorter from the west. So he walked softly before God, smothering his joy down under scowls and muttered curses, and, so, fooling God, for God was the only thing in the universe of which Dan Cullen was afraid.

All Saturday and Saturday night *Mary Rogers* raced her westing. Persistently she logged her fourteen knots, so that by Sunday morning she had covered three hundred and fifty miles. If the wind held, she would make around. If it failed, and the snorter came from anywhere between southwest and north, back the *Mary Rogers* would be hurled and be no better off than she had been seven weeks before. And on Sunday morning the wind was failing. The big sea was going down and running smooth. Both watches were on deck setting sail after sail as fast as the ship could stand it. And now Captain Cullen went around brazenly before God, smoking a big cigar, smiling jubilantly, as if the failing wind delighted him, while down underneath he was raging against God for taking the life out of the blessed wind. *Make westing!* So he would, if God would only leave him alone. Secretly, he pledged himself anew to the Powers of Darkness, if they would let him make westing. He pledged himself so easily because he did not believe in the Powers of Darkness. He really believed only in God, though he did not know it. And in his inverted theology God was really the Prince of Darkness. Captain Cullen was a devil worshipper, but he called the devil by another name, that was all.

At midday, after calling eight bells, Captain Cullen ordered the royals on. The men went aloft faster than they had gone in weeks. Not alone were they nimble because of the westing, but a benignant sun was shining down and limbering their stiff bodies. George Dorety stood aft, near Captain Cullen, less bundled in clothes than usual, soaking in the grateful warmth as he watched the scene. Swiftly and abruptly the incident occurred. There was a cry from the fore-royal yard of "Man overboard!" Somebody threw a life buoy over the side, and at the same instant the second mate's voice came aft, ringing and peremptory:

"Hard down your helm!"

The man at the wheel never moved a spoke. He knew better, for Captain Dan Cullen was standing alongside of him. He wanted to move a spoke, to move all the spokes, to grind the wheel down, hard down, for his comrade drowning in the sea. He glanced at Captain Dan Cullen, and Captain Dan Cullen gave no sign.

"Down! Hard down!" the second mate roared, as he sprang aft.

But he ceased springing and commanding, and stood still, when he saw Dan Cullen by the wheel. And big Dan Cullen puffed at his cigar and said nothing. Astern, and going astern fast, could be seen the sailor. He had caught the life buoy and was clinging to it. Nobody spoke. Nobody moved. The men aloft clung to the royal yards and watched with terror-stricken faces. And the *Mary Rogers* raced on, making her westing. A long, silent minute passed.

"Who was it?" Captain Cullen demanded.

"Mops, sir," eagerly answered the sailor at the wheel.

Mops topped a wave astern and disappeared temporarily in the trough. It was a large wave, but it was no graybeard. A small boat could live easily in such a sea, and in such a sea the *Mary Rogers* could easily come to and make westing at the same time.

For the first time in all his years, George Dorety was seeing a real drama of life and death—a sordid little drama in which the scales balanced an unknown sailor named Mops against a few miles of longitude. At first he had watched the man astern, but now he watched big Dan Cullen, hairy and black, vested with power of life and death, smoking a cigar.

Captain Dan Cullen smoked another long, silent minute. Then he removed the cigar from his mouth. He glanced aloft at the spars of the *Mary Rogers*, and overside at the sea.

"Sheet home the royals!" he cried.

Fifteen minutes later they sat at table, in the cabin, with food served before them. On one side of George Dorety sat Dan Cullen, the tiger, on the other side, Joshua Higgins, the hyena. Nobody spoke. On deck the men were sheeting home the skysails. George Dorety could hear their cries, while a persistent vision haunted him of a man called Mops, alive and well, clinging to a life buoy miles astern in that lonely ocean. He glanced at Captain Cullen, and experienced a feeling of nausea, for the man was eating his food with relish, almost bolting it.

"Captain Cullen," Dorety said, "you're in command of this ship, and it is not proper for me to comment now upon what you do. But I wish to say one thing. There is a hereafter, and yours will be a hot one."

Captain Cullen did not even scowl. In his voice was regret as he said:

"It was blowing a living gale. It was impossible to save the man."

"He fell from the royal yard," Dorety cried hotly. "You were setting the royals at the time. Fifteen minutes afterward you were setting the skysails."

"It was a living gale, wasn't it, Mr. Higgins?" Captain Cullen said, turning to the mate.

"If you'd brought her to, it'd have taken the sticks out of her," was the mate's answer. "You did the proper thing, Captain Cullen. The man hadn't a ghost of a show."

George Dorety made no answer, and to the meal's end no one spoke. After that, Dorety had his meals served in his stateroom. Captain Cullen scowled at him no longer, though no speech was exchanged between them, while the *Mary Rogers* sped north toward warmer latitudes. At the end of the week, Dan Cullen cornered

Dorety on deck.

"What are you going to do when we get to 'Frisco?" he demanded.

"I am going to swear out a warrant for your arrest," Dorety answered quietly. "I am going to charge you with murder, and I am going to see you hanged for it."

"You're almighty sure of yourself," Captain Cullen sneered, turning on his heel.

A second week passed, and one morning found George Dorety standing in the coach house companionway at the for'ard end of the long poop, taking his first gaze around the deck. The *Mary Rogers* was reaching full-and-by, in a stiff breeze. Every sail was set and drawing, including the staysails. Captain Cullen strolled for'ard along the poop. He strolled carelessly, glancing at the passenger out of the corner of his eye. Dorety was looking the other way, standing with head and shoulders outside the companionway, and only the back of his head was to be seen. Captain Cullen, with a swift eye, embraced the mainstaysail-block and the head and estimated the distance. He glanced about him. Nobody was looking. Aft, Joshua Higgins, pacing up and down, had just turned his back and was going the other way. Captain Cullen bent over suddenly and cast the staysail-sheet off from its pin. The heavy block hurtled through the air, smashing Dorety's head like an eggshell and hurtling on and back and forth as the staysail whipped and slatted in the wind. Joshua Higgins turned around to see what had carried away, and met the full blast of the vilest portion of Captain Cullen's profanity.

"I made the sheet fast myself," whimpered the mate in the first lull, "with an extra turn to make sure. I remember it distinctly."

"Made fast?" the captain snarled back, for the benefit of the watch as it struggled to capture the flying sail before it tore to ribbons. "You couldn't make your grandmother fast, you useless hell's scullion. If you made that sheet fast with an extra turn, why in hell didn't it stay fast? That's what I want to know. Why in hell didn't it stay fast?"

The mate whined inarticulately.

"Oh shut up!" was the final word of Captain Cullen.

Half an hour later he was as surprised as any when the body of George Dorety was found inside the companionway on the floor. In the afternoon, alone in his room, he doctored up the log.

"Ordinary seaman, Karl Brun," he wrote, "lost overboard from fore-royal yard in a gale of wind. Was running at the time, and for the safety of the ship did not dare come up to the wind. Nor could a boat have lived in the sea that was running."

On another page, he wrote:

"Had often warned Mr. Dorety about the danger he ran because of his carelessness on deck. I told him, once, that some day he would get his head knocked off by a block. A carelessly fastened mainstaysail-sheet was the cause of the accident, which was deeply to be regretted because Mr. Dorety was a favorite with all of us."

Captain Dan Cullen read over his literary effort with admiration, blotted the page, and closed the log. He lighted a cigar and stared before him. He felt the Mary Rogers lift, and heel, and surge along, and knew that she was making nine knots. A smile of satisfaction slowly dawned on his black and hairy face. Well, anyway, he had made his westing and fooled God.

Born in San Francisco possibly as an illegitimate son of an itinerant astrologer, Jack London (1876–1916) grew up tough and lawless and was an oyster pirate by age fifteen. He tells brutal tales of the sea and of the gold rush in the Klondike, and is best known for his novel Call of the Wild *(1903), as well as many other adventure stories. This tale is from* When God Laughs *(1911).*

THE NEW YORK WATERFRONT IN 1828

The Open Boat

Stephen Crane

A tale intended to be after the fact: being the experience of four men from the sunk steamer *Commodore*.

I

None of them knew the color of the sky. Their eyes glanced level and were fastened upon the waves that swept toward them. These waves were of the hue of slate, save for the tops, which were of foaming white, and all of the men knew the color of the sea. The horizon narrowed and widened, and dipped and rose, and at all times its edge was jagged with waves that seemed thrust up in points like rocks.

Many a man ought to have a bathtub larger than the boat which he rode upon the sea. These waves were most wrongfully and barbarously abrupt and tall, and each froth-top was a problem in a small-boat navigation.

The cook squatted in the bottom, and looked with both eyes at the six inches of gunwale which separated him from the ocean. His sleeves were rolled over his fat forearms, and the two flaps of his unbuttoned hand dangled as he bent to bail out the boat. Often he said, "Gawd! that was a narrow clip." As he remarked it he invariably gazed eastward over the broken sea.

The oiler, steering with one of the two oars in the boat, some-times raised himself suddenly to keep clear of water that swirled in over the stern. It was a thin little oar, and it seemed often ready to snap.

The correspondent, pulling at the other oar, watched the waves and wondered why he was there.

The injured captain, lying in the bow, was at this time buried in that profound dejection and indifference which comes, temporarily at least, to even the bravest and most enduring when, willy-nilly, the firm fails, the army loses, the ship goes down. The mind of the master of a vessel is rooted deep in the timbers of her, though he command for a day or a decade; and this captain had on him the stern impression of a scene in the grays of dawn of seven turned faces, and later a stump of a topmast with a white ball on it, that slashed to and fro at the waves, went low and lower, and down. Thereafter there was something strange in his voice. Although steady, it was deep with mourning, and of a quality beyond oration or tears.

"Keep 'er a little more south, Billie," said he.

"A little more south, sir," said the oiler in the stern.

A seat in this boat was not unlike a seat upon a bucking bronco, and by the same token a bronco is not much smaller. As each wave came, and she rose for it, she seemed like a horse making at a fence outrageously high. The manner of her scramble over these walls of water is a mystic thing, and, moreover, at the top of them were ordinarily these problems in white water, the foam racing down from the summit of each wave requiring a new leap, and a leap from the air. Then, after scornfully bumping a crest, she would slide and race and splash down a long incline, and arrive bobbing and nodding in front of the next menace.

A singular disadvantage of the sea lies in the fact that after successfully surmounting one wave you discover that there is another behind it just as important and just as nervously anxious to do something effective in the way of swamping boats. In a ten-foot dinghy one can get an idea of the resources of the sea in the line of waves that is not probable to the average experience, which is never at sea in a dinghy. As each slaty wall of water approached, it shut all else from the views of the men of the boat, and it was not difficult to imagine that this particular wave was the final outburst of the ocean, the last effort of the grim water. There was a terrible grace in the move of the waves, and they came in silence, save for the snarling of the crests.

In the wan light the faces of the men must have been gray. Their eyes must have glinted in strange ways as they gazed steadily astern. Viewed from a balcony, the whole thing would, doubtless, have been weirdly picturesque. But the men in the boat had no time to see it, and if they had had leisure, there were other things to occupy their minds. The sun swung steadily up the sky, and they knew it was broad day because the color of the sea changed from slate to emerald green streaked with amber lights, and the foam was like tumbling snow. The process of the breaking day was unknown to them. They were aware only of this effect upon the color of the waves that rolled toward them.

In disjointed sentences the cook and the correspondent argued as to the difference between a lifesaving station and a house of refuge. The cook had said: "There's a house of refuge just north of the Mosquito Inlet Light, as soon as they see us they'll come off in their boat and pick us up."

"As soon as who see us?" said the correspondent.

"Houses of refuge don't have crews," said the correspondent. "As I understand them, they are the only places where clothes and grub are stored for the benefit of shipwrecked people. They don't carry crews."

"Oh, yes, they do," said the cook.

"No, they don't," said the correspondent.

"Well, we're not there yet, anyhow," said the oiler, in the stern.

"Well," said the cook, "perhaps it's not a house of refuge that I'm thinking of as being near Mosquito Inlet Light; perhaps it's a lifesaving station."

"We're not there yet," said the oiler in the stern.

II

As the boat bounced from the top of the each wave the wind tore through the hair of the hatless men, and as the craft plopped her stern down again the spray splashed past them. The crest of each of these waves was a hill, from the top of which the men surveyed for a moment a broad tumultuous expanse, shining and wind-riven. It was probably splendid, it was probably glorious, this play of the free sea, wild with lights of emerald and white and amber.

"Bully good thing it's an onshore wind," said the cook. "If not, where would we be? Wouldn't have a show."

"That's right," said the correspondent.

The busy oiler nodded his assent.

Then the captain, in the bow, chuckled in a way that expressed humor, contempt, tragedy, all in one. "Do you think we've got much of a show now, boys?" said he.

Whereupon the three were silent, save for a trifle of hemming and hawing. To express any particular optimism at this time they felt to be childish and stupid, but they all doubtless possessed this sense of the situations in their minds. A young man thinks doggedly at such times. On the other hand, the ethics of their condition was decidedly against any open suggestion of hopelessness. So they were silent.

"Oh, well," said the captain, soothing his children, "we'll get ashore all right."

But there was that in his tone which made them think; so the oiler quoth, "Yes! if this wind holds."

The cook was bailing. "Yes! if we don't catch hell in the surf."

Canton-flannel gulls flew near and far. Sometimes they sat down on the sea, near patches of brown seaweed that rolled over the waves with a movement like carpets on a line in a gale. The birds sat comfortably in groups, and they were envied by some in the dinghy, for the wrath of the sea was no more to them than it was to a covey of prairie chickens a thousand miles inland. Often they came very close and stared at the men with black bead-like eyes. At these times they were uncanny and sinister in their unblinking scrutiny, and the men hooted angrily at them, telling them to be gone. One came, and evidently decided to alight on the top of the captain's head. The bird flew parallel to the boat and did not circle, but made short sidelong jumps in the air in chicken fashion. His black eyes were wistfully fixed upon the captain's head. "Ugly brute," said the oiler to the bird. "You look as if you were made with a jack-knife." The cook and the correspondent swore darkly at the creature. The captain naturally wished to knock it away with the end of the heavy painter, but he did not dare do it, because anything resembling an emphatic gesture would have capsized this freighted boat; and so, with his open hand, the captain gently and carefully waved the gull away. After it had been discouraged from the pursuit the captain breathed easier on account of his hair, and others breathed easier because the bird struck their minds at this time as being somehow gruesome and ominous.

In the meantime the oiler and the correspondent rowed; and also they rowed. They sat together in the same seat, and each rowed an oar. Then the oiler took both oars; then the correspondent took both oars, then the oiler; then the correspondent. They rowed and they rowed. The very ticklish part of the business was when the time came for the reclining one in the stern to take his turn at the oars. By the very last star of truth, it is easier to steal eggs from under a hen than it was to change seats in the dinghy. First the man in the stern slid his hand along the thwart and moved with care, as if he were of Sèvres. Then the man in the rowing seat slid his hand along the other thwart. It was all done with the most extraordinary care. As the two sidled past each other, the whole party kept watchful eyes on the coming wave, and the captain cried: "Look out, now! Steady, there!"

The brown mats of seaweed that appeared from time to time were like islands, bits of earth. They were travelling, apparently, neither one way nor the other. They were, to all intents, stationary. They informed the men in the boat that it was making progress slowly toward the land. The captain, rearing cautiously in the bow after the dinghy soared on a great swell, said that he had seen the lighthouse at Mosquito Inlet. Presently the cook remarked that he had seen it. The correspondent was at the oars then, and for some reason he too wished to look at the lighthouse, but his back was toward the far shore, and the waves were important, and for some time he could not seize an opportunity to turn his head. But at last there came a wave more gentle than the others, and when at the crest of it he swiftly scoured the western horizon.

"See it?" said the captain.

"No," said the correspondent, slowly: "I didn't see anything."

"Look again," said the captain. He pointed. "It's exactly in that direction."

At the top of another wave the correspondent did as he was bid, and this time his eyes chanced on a small, still thing on the edge of the swaying horizon. It was precisely like the point of a pin. It took an anxious eye to find a lighthouse so tiny.

"Think we'll make it, Captain?"

"If this wind holds and the boat don't swamp, we can't do much else," said the captain.

The little boat, lifted by each towering sea and splashed viciously by the crests, made progress that in the absence of seaweed was not apparent to those in her. She seemed just a wee thing wallowing, miraculously top up, at the mercy of five oceans. Occasionally a great spread of water, like white flames, swarmed into her.

"Bail her, cook," said the captain, serenely.

"All right, Captain." said the cheerful cook.

III

It would be difficult to describe the subtle brotherhood of men that was here established on the seas. No one said that it was so. No one mentioned it. But it dwelt in the boat, and each man felt it warm him. They were a captain, an oiler, a cook, and a correspondent, and they were friends—friends in a more curiously iron-bound degree than may be common. The hurt captain, lying against the water jar in the bow, spoke always in a low voice and calmly; but he could never command a more ready and swiftly obedient crew than the motley three of the dinghy. It was more than a mere recognition of what was best for the common safety. There was surely in it a quality that was personal and heartfelt. And after this devotion to the commander of the boat, there was this comradeship, that the correspondent, for instance, who had been taught to be cynical of men, knew even at the time was the best experience of his life. But no one said that it was so. No one mentioned it.

"I wish we had a sail," remarked the captain. "We might try my overcoat on the end of an oar, and give you two boys a chance to rest." So the cook and the correspondent held the mast and spread wide the overcoat; the oiler steered; and the little boat made good way with her new rig. Sometimes the oiler had to scull sharply to keep a sea from breaking into the boat, but otherwise sailing was a success.

Meanwhile the lighthouse had been growing slowly larger. It had now almost assumed color, and appeared like a little gray shadow on the sky. The man at the oars could not be prevented from turning his head rather often to try for a glimpse of this little gray shadow.

At last, from the top of each wave, the men in the tossing boat could see land. Even as the lighthouse was an upright shadow on the sky, this land seemed but a long black shadow on the sea. It certainly was thinner than paper. "We must be about opposite New Smyrna," said the cook, who had coasted this shore often in schooners. "Captain, by the way, I believe they abandoned that lifesaving station there about a year ago."

"Did they?" said the captain.

The wind slowly died away. The cook and the correspondent were not now obliged to slave in order to hold high the oar. But the waves continued their old impetuous swooping at the dinghy, and the little craft, no longer underway, struggled woundily over them. The oiler or the correspondent took the oars again.

Shipwrecks are apropos of nothing. If men could only train for them and have them occur when the men had reached pink condition, there would be less drowning at sea. Of the four in the dinghy none had slept any time worth mentioning for two days and two nights previous to embarking in the dinghy, and in the excitement of clambering about the deck of a foundering ship they had also forgotten to eat heartily.

For these reasons, and for others, neither the oiler nor the correspondent was fond of rowing at this time. The correspondent wondered ingenuously how in the name of all that was sane could there be people who thought it amusing to row a boat. It was not an amusement; it was a diabolical punishment, and even a genius of mental aberrations could never conclude that it was anything but a horror to the muscles and a crime against the back. He mentioned to the boat in general how the amusement of rowing struck him, and the weary-faced oiler smiled in full sympathy. Previously to the foundering, by the way, the oiler had worked a double watch in the engine room.

"Take her easy now, boys," said the captain. "Don't spend yourselves. If we have to run a surf you'll need all your strength, because we'll sure have to swim for it. Take your time."

Slowly the land arose from the sea. From a black line it became a line of black and a line of white—trees and sand. Finally the captain said that he could make out a house on the shore. "That's the house of refuge, sure," said the cook. "They'll see us before long, and come out after us."

The distant lighthouse reared high. "The keeper ought to be able to make us out now, if he's looking through a glass," said the captain. "He'll notify the lifesaving people."

"None of those other boats could have got ashore to give word of this wreck," said the oiler, in a low voice, "else the lifeboat would be out hunting us."

Slowly and beautifully the land loomed out of the sea. The wind came again. It had veered from the northeast to the southeast. Finally a new sound struck the ears of the men in the boat. It was the low thunder of the surf on the shore. "We'll never be able to make the lighthouse now," said the captain. "Swing her head a little more north, Billie."

"A little more north, sir," said the oiler.

Whereupon the little boat turned her nose once more down the wind, and all but the oarsman watched the shore grow. Under the influence of this expansion, doubt and direful apprehension were leaving the minds of the men. The management of the boat was still most absorbing, but it could not prevent a quiet cheerfulness. In an hour, perhaps, they would be ashore.

Their backbones had become thoroughly used to

balancing in the boat, and they now rode this wild colt of a dinghy like circus men. The correspondent thought that he had been drenched to the skin, but happening to feel in the top pocket of his coat, he found therein eight cigars. Four of them were soaked with seawater; four were perfectly scatheless. After a search, somebody produced three dry matches; and thereupon the four waifs rode impudently in their little boat and, with an assurance of impending rescue shining in their eyes, puffed at the big cigars, and judged well and ill of all men. Everybody took a drink of water.

IV

"Cook," remarked the captain, "there don't seem to be any signs of life about your house of refuge."

"No," replied the cook. "Funny they don't see us!"

A broad stretch of lowly coast lay before the eyes of the men. It was of low dunes topped with dark vegetation. The roar of the surf was plain, and sometimes they could see the white lip of a wave as it spun up the beach. A tiny house was blocked out black upon the sky. Southward, the slim lighthouse lifted its little gray length.

Tide, wind, and waves were swinging the dinghy northward. "Funny they don't see us," said the men.

The surf's roar was here dulled, but its tone was nevertheless thunderous and mighty. As the boat swam over the great rollers the men sat listening to this roar. "We'll swamp sure," said everybody.

It is fair to say here that there was not a lifesaving station within twenty miles in either direction; but the men did not know this fact, and in consequence they made the dark and opprobious remarks concerning the eyesight of the nation's lifesavers. Four scowling men sat in the dinghy and surpassed records in the invention of epithets.

"Funny they don't see us."

The lightheartedness of the former time had completely faded. To their sharpened minds it was easy to conjure pictures of all kinds of incompetency and blindness and, indeed, cowardice. There was the shore of the populous land, and it was bitter and bitter to them that from it came no sign.

"Well," said the captain, ultimately, "I suppose we'll have to make a try for ourselves. If we stay out here too long, we'll none of us have strength left to swim after the boat swamps."

And so the oiler, who was at the oars, turned the boat straight for the shore. There was a sudden tightening of muscles. There was some thinking. "If we don't all get ashore," said the captain—"if we don't all get ashore, I suppose you fellows know where to send news of my finish?"

They then briefly exchanged some addresses and admonitions. As for the reflections of the men, there was a great deal of rage in them. Perchance they might be formulated thus: "If I am going to be drowned—if I am going to be drowned—if I am going to be drowned, why, in the name of the seven mad gods who rule the sea, was I allowed to come thus far and contemplate sand and trees? Was I brought here merely to have my nose dragged away as I was about to nibble the sacred cheese of life? It is preposterous. If this old ninny-woman, Fate, cannot do better than this, she should be deprived of the management of men's fortunes. She is an old hen who knows not her intention. If she has decided to drown me, why did she not do it in the beginning and save me all this trouble? The whole affair is absurd. . . . But no; she cannot mean to drown me. She dare not drown me. She cannot drown me. Not after all this work." Afterward the man might have had an impulse to shake his fist at the clouds. "Just you drown me, now, and then hear what I call you!"

The billows that came at this time were more formidable. They seemed always just about to break and roll over the little boat in a turmoil of foam. There was a preparatory and long growl in the speech of them. No mind unused to the sea would have concluded that the dinghy could ascend these sheer heights in time. The shore was still afar. The oiler was a wily surfman. "Boys," he said swiftly, "she won't live three minutes more, and we're too far out to swim. Shall I take her to sea again, Captain?"

"Yes, go ahead!" said the captain.

This oiler, by a series of quick miracles and fast and steady oarsmanship, turned the boat in the middle of the surf and took her safely to sea again.

There was a considerable silence as the boat bumped over the furrowed sea to deeper water. Then somebody in gloom spoke: "Well, anyhow, they must have seen us from the shore by now."

The gulls went in slanting flight up the wind to-

"THE MARINER'S REST," AN ILLUSTRATION FROM MID-NINETEENTH CENTURY SHEET MUSIC

ward the gray, desolate east. A squall, marked by dingy clouds and clouds brick-red, like smoke from a burning building, appeared from the southeast.

"What do you think of those lifesaving people? Ain't they peaches?"

"Funny they haven't seen us."

"Maybe they think we're out here for sport! Maybe they think we're fishin'. Maybe they think we're damned fools "

It was a long afternoon. A changed tide tried to force them southward but wind and wave said northward. Far ahead, where coastline, sea, and sky formed their mighty angle, there were little dots which seemed to indicate a city on the shore.

"St. Augustine?"

The captain shook his head. "Too near Mosquito Inlet." And the oiler rowed, and then the correspondent rowed; then the oiler rowed. It was a weary busi-

ness. The human back can become the seat of more aches and pains than are registered in books for the composite anatomy of a regiment. It is a limited area, but it can become the theater of innumerable muscular conflicts, tangles, wrenches, knots, and other discomforts.

"Did you ever like to row, Billie?" asked the correspondent.

"No." said the oiler, "hang it!"

When one exchanged the rowing seat for a place in the bottom of the boat, he suffered a bodily depression that caused him to be careless of everything save an obligation to wiggle one finger. There was cold seawater swashing to and fro in the boat, and he lay in it. His head, pillowed on a thwart, was within an inch of the swirl of a wave-crest, and sometimes a particularly obstreperous sea came inboard and drenched him once more. But these matters did not annoy him. It is almost certain that if the boat had capsized he would have tumbled comfortably out upon the ocean as if he felt sure that it was a great soft mattress.

"Look! There's a man on the shore!"

"Where?"

"There! See 'im? See 'im?"

"Yes, sure! He's walking along."

"Now he's stopped. Look! He's facing us!"

"He's waving at us!"

"So he is! By thunder!"

"Ah, now we're all right! Now we're all right! There'll be a boat out here for us in half an hour."

"He's going on. He's running. He's going up to that house there."

The remote beach seemed lower than the sea, and it required a searching glance to discern the little black figure. The captain saw a floating stick, and they rowed to it. A bath towel was by some weird chance in the boat, and, tying this on the stick, the captain waved it. The oarsman did not dare turn his head, so he was obliged to ask questions.

"What's he doing now?"

"He's standing still again. He's looking, I think. . . . There he goes again—toward the house. . . . Now he's stopped again."

"Is he waving at us?"

"No, not now; he was, though."

"Look! There comes another man!"

"He's running."

"Look at him go, would you!"

"Why, he's on a bicycle. Now he's met the other man. They're both waving at us. Look!"

"There comes something up the beach."

"What the devil is that thing?"

"Why, it looks like a boat."

"Why, certainly, it's a boat."

"No, its on wheels."

"Yes so it is. Well, that must be the lifeboat. They drag them along shore on a wagon."

"That's the lifeboat, sure."

"No, by God, it's—it's an omnibus."

"I tell you it's a lifeboat."

"It is not! It's an omnibus. I can see it plain. See? One of these big hotel omnibuses."

"By thunder, you're right. It's an omnibus, sure as fate. What do you suppose they are doing with an om-

nibus? Maybe they are going around collecting the life-crew, hey?"

"That's it, likely. Look! There's a fellow waving a little black flag. He's standing on the steps of the omnibus. There come those other two fellows. Now they're all talking together. Look at the fellow with the flag. Maybe he ain't waving it!"

"That ain't a flag, is it? That's his coat. Why, certainly, that's his coat."

"So it is; it's his coat. He's taken it off and is waving it around his head. But would you look at him swing it!"

"Oh say, there isn't any lifesaving station there. That's just a winter-resort hotel omnibus that has brought over some of the boarders to see us drown."

"What's that idiot with the coat mean? What's he signaling, anyhow?"

"It looks as if he were trying to tell us to go north. There must be a lifesaving station up there."

"No; he thinks we're fishing. Just giving us a merry hand. See? Ah, there Willie!"

"Well, I wish I could make something out of those signals. What do you suppose he means?"

"He don't mean anything; he's just playing."

"Well, if he'd just signal us to try the surf again, or to go to sea and wait, or go north, or go south, or go to hell, there would be some reason in it. But look at him! He just stands there and keeps his coat revolving like a wheel. The ass!"

"There come more people."

"Now there's quite a mob. Look! Isn't that a boat?"

"Where? Oh, I see where you mean. No, that's no boat."

"That fellow is still waving his coat."

"He must think we like to see him do that. Why don't he quit it? It don't mean anything."

"I don't know. I think he is trying to make us go north. It must be that there's a lifesaving station there somewhere."

"Say, he ain't tired yet. Look at 'im wave!"

"Wonder how long he can keep that up. He's been revolving his coat ever since he caught sight of us. He's an idiot. Why aren't they getting men to bring a boat out? A fishing boat—one of those big yawls—could come out here all right. Why don't he do something?"

"Oh, it's all right now."

"They'll have a boat out here for us in less than no

time, now that they've seen us."

A faint yellow tone came into the sky over the low land. The shadows on the sea slowly deepened. The wind bore coldness with it, and the men began to shiver.

"Holy smoke!" said one, allowing his voice to express his impious mood "if we keep on monkeying out here! If we've got to flounder out here all night!"

"Oh, we'll never have to stay here all night! Don't you worry. They've seen us now, and it won't be long before they'll come chasing out after us."

The shore grew dusky. The man waving the coat blended gradually into this gloom, and it swallowed in the same manner the omnibus and the group of people. The spray, when it dashed uproariously over the side, made the voyagers shrink and swear like men who were being branded.

"I'd like to catch the chump who waved the coat. I feel like socking him one, just for luck."

"Why? What did he do?"

"Oh, nothing, but then he seemed so damn cheerful."

In the meantime the oiler rowed, and then the correspondent rowed, and then the oiler rowed. Grayfaced and bowed forward, they mechanically, turn by turn, plied the leaden oars. The form of the lighthouse had vanished fron the southern horizon, but finally a pale star appeared, just lifting from the sea. The streaked saffron in the west passed before the all-merging darkness, and the sea to the east was black. The land had vanished, and was expressed only by the low and drear thunder of the surf.

"If I am going to be drowned—if I am going to be drowned—if I am going to be drowned, why, in the name of the seven mad gods who rule the sea, was I allowed to come thus far and contemplate sand and trees? Was I brought here merely to have my nose dragged away as I was about to nibble the sacred cheese of life?"

The patient captain, drooped over the water jar, was sometimes obliged to speak to the oarsman.

"Keep her head up! Keep her head up!"

"Keep her head up, sir." The voices were weary and low.

This was surely a quiet evening. All save the oarsman lay heavily and listlessly in the boat's bottom. As for him, his eyes were just capable of noting the tall black waves that swept forward in a most sinister silence, save for an occasional subdued growl of a crest.

The cook's head was on a thwart, and he looked without interest at the water under his nose. He was deep in other scenes. Finally he spoke. "Billie," he murmured, dreamfully, "what kind of pie do you like best?"

V

"Pie!" said the oiler and the correspondent, agitatedly. "Don't talk about those things, blast you!"

"Well," said the cook. "I was just thinking about ham sandwiches, and—"

A night on the sea in an open boat is a long night. As darkness settled finally, the shine of the light, lifting from the sea in the south, changed to full gold. On the northern horizon a new light appeared, a small bluish gleam on the edge of the waters. These two lights were the furniture of the world. Otherwise there was nothing but waves.

Two men were huddled in the stern, and distances were so magnificent in the dinghy that the rower was enabled to keep his feet partly warm by thrusting them under his companions. Their legs indeed extended far under the rowing seat until they touched the feet of the captain forward. Sometimes, despite the efforts of the tired oarsman, a wave came piling into the boat, an icy wave of the night, and the chilling water soaked them anew. They would twist their bodies for a moment and groan, and sleep the deep sleep once more, while the water in the boat gurgled about them as the craft rocked.

The plan of the oiler and the correspondent was for one to row until he lost the ability, and then arouse the other from his seawater couch in the bottom of the boat. The oiler plied the oars until his head drooped forward and the overpowering sleep blinded him; and he rowed yet afterward. Then he touched a man in the bottom of the boat, and called his name. "Will you spell me for a little while?" he said meekly.

"Sure, Billie," said the correspondent, awaking and dragging himself to a sitting position. They exchanged places carefully, and the oiler, cuddling down in the seawater at the cook's side, seemed to go to sleep instantly.

The particular violence of the sea had ceased. The

waves came without snarling. The obligation of the man at the oars was to keep the boat headed so that the tilt of the rollers would not capsize her, and to preserve her from filling when the crests rushed past. The black waves were silent and hard to be seen in the darkness. Often one was almost upon the boat before the oarsman was aware.

In a low voice the correspondent addressed the captain. He was not sure that the captain was awake, although this iron man seemed to be always awake. "Captain, shall I keep her making for that light north, sir?"

The same steady voice answered him. "Yes. Keep it about two points off the port bow."

The cook had tied a life-belt around himself in order to get even the warmth which this clumsy cork contrivance could donate, and he seemed almost stove-like when a rower, whose teeth invariably chattered wildly as soon as he ceased his labor, dropped down to sleep.

The correspondent, as he rowed, looked down at the two men sleeping underfoot. The cook's arm was around the oiler's shoulders, and, with their fragmentary clothing and haggard faces, they were the babes of the sea—a grotesque rendering of the old babes in the wood.

Later he must have grown stupid at his work, for suddenly there was a growling of water, and a crest came with a roar and a swash into the boat, and it was a wonder that it did not set the cook afloat in his life-belt. The cook continued to sleep, but the oiler sat up, blinking his eyes and shaking with the new cold.

"Oh, I'm awful sorry, Billie," said the correspondent, contritely.

"That's all right, old boy," said the oiler, and lay down again and was asleep.

Presently it seemed that even the captain dozed, and the correspondent thought that he was the one man afloat on all the ocean. The wind had a voice as it came over the waves, and it was sadder than the end.

There was a long, loud swishing astern of the boat, and a gleaming trail of phosphorescence, like blue flame, was furrowed on the black waters. It might have been made by a monstrous knife.

Then there came a stillness, while the correspondent breathed with open mouth and looked at the sea.

Suddenly there was another swish and another long

flash of bluish light and this time it was alongside the boat, and might almost have been reached with an oar. The correspondent saw an enormous fin speed like a shadow through the water, hurling the crystalline spray and leaving the long glowing trail.

The correspondent looked over his shoulder at the captain. His face was hidden, and he seemed to be asleep. He looked at the babes of the sea. They certainly were asleep. So, being bereft of sympathy, he leaned a little way to one side and swore softly into the sea.

But the thing did not then leave the vicinity of the boat. Ahead or astern, on one side or the other, at intervals long or short, fled the long sparkling streak, and there was to be heard the *whirroo* of the dark fin. The speed and power of the thing was greatly to be admired. It cut the water like a gigantic and keen projectile.

The presence of this biding thing did not affect the man with the same horror that it would if he had been a picnicker. He simply looked at the sea dully and swore in an undertone.

Nevertheless, it is true that he did not wish to be alone with the thing. He wished one of his companions to awake by chance and keep him company with it. But the captain hung motionless over the water jar, and the oiler and the cook in the bottom of the boat were plunged in slumber.

VI

"If I am going to be drowned—if I am going to be drowned—if I am going to be drowned, why, in the name of the seven mad gods who rule the sea, was I allowed to come thus far and contemplate sand and trees?"

During this dismal night, it may be remarked that a man would conclude that it was really the intention of the seven mad gods to drown him, despite the abominable injustice of it. For it was certainly an abominable injustice to drown a man who had worked so hard, so hard. The man felt it would be a crime most unnatural. Other people had drowned at sea since galleys swarmed with painted sails, but still. . . .

When it occurs to a man that nature does not regard him as important, and that she feels she would not maim the universe by disposing of him, he at first wishes to throw bricks at the temple, and he hates deeply

"MAN THE LIFEBOAT," AN ILLUSTRATION FROM MID-NINETEENTH CENTURY SHEET MUSIC

the fact that there are no bricks and no temples. Any visible expression of nature would surely be pelleted with his jeers.

Then, if there be no tangible thing to hoot, he feels, perhaps, the desire to confront a personification and indulge in pleas, bowed to one knee, and with hands supplicant, saying, "Yes, but I love myself."

A high cold star on a winter's night is the word he feels that she says to him. Thereafter he knows the pathos of his situation.

The men in the dinghy had not discussed these matters, but each had, no doubt, reflected upon them in silence and according to his mind. There was seldom any expression upon their faces save the general one of complete weariness. Speech was devoted to the business of the boat.

To chime the notes of his emotion, a verse mysteriously entered the correspondent's head. He had even forgotten that he had forgotten this verse, but it suddenly was in his mind.

A soldier of the legion lay dying in Algiers;
There was lack of woman's nursing,
    there was dearth of woman's tears;
But a comrade stood beside him,
    and he took the comrade's hand,
And he said, "I never more shall see
    my own, my native land."

In his childhood the correspondent had been made acquainted with the fact that a soldier of the Legion lay dying in Algiers, but he had never regarded it as important. Myriads of his schoolfellows had informed him of the soldier's plight, but the dinning had naturally ended by making him perfectly indifferent. He had never considered it his affair that a soldier of the Legion lay dying in Algiers, nor had it appeared to him as a matter for sorrow. It was less to him than the breaking of a pencil's point.

Now, however, it quaintly came to him as a human, living thing. It was no longer merely a picture of a few throes in the breast of a poet, meanwhile drinking tea and warming his feet at the grate; it was an actuality—stern, mournful, and fine.

The correspondent plainly saw the soldier. He lay on the sand with his feet out straight and still. While his pale left hand was upon his chest in attempt to thwart the going of his life, the blood came between his fingers. In the far Algerian distance, a city of low square forms was set against a sky that was faint with the last sunset hues. The correspondent, plying the oars and dreaming of the slow and slower movements of the lips of the soldier's moved by a profound and perfectly impersonal comprehension. He was sorry for the soldier of the Legion who lay dying in Algiers.

The thing which had followed the boat and waited had evidently grown tired at the delay. There was no longer to be heard the slash of the cutter, and there was no longer the flame of the long trail. The light in the path still glimmered, but it was apparently no nearer to the boat. Sometimes the boom of the surf rang in the correspondent's ears, and he turned the craft seaward then and rowed harder. Southward, some one had evidently built a watch fire on the beach. It was too low and too far to be seen, it made a shimmering, roseate reflection upon the bluff in back of it, and this could be discerned from the boat. The wind came stronger, and sometimes a wave suddenly raged out like a mountain-cat, and there was to be seen the sheen and sparkle of a broken crest.

The captain, in the bow, moved on his water jar and sat erect. "Pretty long night," he observed to the correspondent. He looked at the shore. "Those lifesaving people take their time."

"Did you see that shark playing around?"

"Yes, I saw him. He was a big fellow, all right."

"Wish I had known you were awake."

Later the correspondent spoke into the bottom of the boat. "Billie!" There was a slow and gradual disentanglement. "Billie, will you spell me?"

"Sure," said the oiler.

As soon as the correspondent touched the cold, comfortable seawater in the bottom of the boat and had huddled close to the cook's life-belt he was deep in sleep, despite the fact that his teeth played all the popular airs. This sleep was so good to him that it was but a moment before he heard a voice call his name in a tone that demonstrated the last stages of exhaustion. "Will you spell me?"

"Sure, Billie."

The light in the north had mysteriously vanished, but the correspondent took his course from the wide-awake captain.

Later in the night they took the boat farther out to sea, and the captain directed the cook to take one oar at the stern and keep the boat facing the seas. He was to call out if he should hear the thunder of the surf. This plan enabled the oiler and the correspondent to get respite together. "We'll give those boys a chance to get into shape again," said the captain. They curled down and, after a few preliminary chatterings and trembles, slept once more the dead sleep. Neither knew they had bequeathed to the cook the company of another shark, or perhaps the same shark.

As the boat caroused on the waves, spray occasionally bumped over the side and gave them a fresh soaking, but this had no power to break their repose. The ominous slash of the wind and the water affected them as it would have affected mummies.

"Boys," said the cook, with the notes of every reluctance in his voice, "she's drifted in pretty close. I guess one of you had better take her to sea again." The correspondent, aroused, heard the crash of the toppled crests.

As he was rowing, the captain gave him some whiskey and water, and this steadied the chills out of him. "If I ever get ashore and anybody shows me even a photograph of an oar—"

At last there was a short conversation.

"Billie! . . . Billie, will you spell me?"

"Sure," said the oiler.

VII

When the correspondent again opened his eyes, the sky and the sea were each of the gray hue of the dawning. Later, carmine and gold was painted upon the waters. The morning appeared finally, in its splendor, with a sky of pure blue, and the sunlight flamed on the tips of the waves.

On the distant dunes were set many little black cottages, and a tall white windmill reared above them. No man, nor dog, nor bicycle appeared on the beach. The cottages might have formed a deserted village.

The voyagers scanned the shore. A conference was held in the boat. "Well," said the captain, "if no help is coming, we might better try a run through the surf right away. If we stay out here much longer we will be too weak to do anything for ourselves at all." The others silently acquiesced in this reasoning. The boat was headed for the beach. The correspondent wondered if none ever ascended the tall wind tower, and if then they never looked seaward. This tower was a giant, standing with its back to the plight of the ants. It represented in a degree, to the correspondent, the serenity of nature amid the struggles of the individual—nature in the wind, and nature in the vision of men. She did not seem cruel to him then, nor beneficent, nor treacherous, nor wise. But she was indifferent, flatly indifferent. It is, perhaps, plausible that a man in this situation, impressed with the unconcern of the universe, should see the innumerable flaws of his life, and have them taste wickedly in his mind, and wish for another chance. A distinction between right and wrong seems absurdly clear to him, then, in this new ignorance of the grave-edge, and he understands that if he were given another opportunity he would mend his conduct and his words would be better and brighter during an introduction or at a tea.

"Now, boys," said the captain, "she is going to swamp sure. All we can do is to work her in as far as possible, and then when she swamps, pile out and scramble for the beach. Keep cool now, and don't jump until she swamps sure."

The oiler took the oars. Over his shoulders he scanned the surf.

"Captain," he said, "I think I'd better bring her about and keep her head-on to the seas and back her in."

"All right, Billie," said the captain. "Back her in." The oiler swung the boat then, and, seated in the stern, the cook and the correspondent were obliged to contemplate the lonely and indifferent shore.

The monstrous inshore rollers heaved the boat high until the men were again enabled to see the white sheets of water scudding up the slanted beach. "We won't get in very close," said the captain. Each time a man could wrest his attention from the rollers, he turned his glance toward the shore, and in the expression of his eyes during the contemplation there was a singular quality. The correspondent, observing the others, knew that they were not afraid, but the full meaning of their glances was shrouded.

As for himself, he was too tired to grapple fundamentally with the fact. He tried to coerce his mind into thinking of it, but the mind was dominated at this time by the muscles, and the muscles said they did not care. It merely occured to him that if he should drown it would be a shame.

There were no hurried words, no pallor, no plain agitation. The men simply looked at the shore. "Now, remember to get well clear of the boat when you jump," said the captain.

Seaward the crest of a roller suddenly fell with a thunderous crash, and the long white comber came roaring down upon the boat.

"Steady now," said the captain. The men were silent. They turned their eyes from the shore to the comber and waited. The boat slid up the incline, leaped at the furious top, bounced over it, and swung down the long back of the wave. Some water had been shipped, and the cook bailed it out.

But the next crest crashed also. The tumbling, boiling flood of white water caught the boat and whirled it almost perpendicular. Water swarmed in from all sides. The correspondent had his hands on the gunwale at this time, and when the water entered at that place he swiftly withdrew his fingers, as if he objected to wetting them.

The little boat, drunken with this weight of water, reeled and snuggled deeper into the sea.

"Bail her out, cook! Bail her out!" said the captain.

"All right, Captain," said the cook.

"Now, boys, the next one will do us for sure," said the oiler. "Mind to jump clear of the boat."

The third wave moved forward, huge, furious, implacable. It fairly swallowed the dinghy, and almost simultaneously the men tumbled into the sea. A piece of life-belt had lain in the bottom of the boat, and as the correspondent went overboard he held this to his chest with his left hand.

The January water was icy, and reflected immediately that it was colder than he had expected to find off the coast of Florida. This appeared to his dazed mind as a fact important enough to be noted at the time. The coldness of the water was sad; it was tragic. This fact was somehow mixed and confused with his opinion of his own situation, so that it seemed almost a proper reason for tears. The water was cold.

When he came to the surface he was conscious of little but the noisy water. Afterward he saw his companions in the sea. The oiler was ahead in the race. He was swimming strongly and rapidly. Off to the correspondent's left, the cook's great white and corked back bulged out of the water, and in the rear the captain was hanging with his one good hand to the keel of the overturned dinghy.

There is a certain immovable quality to a shore, and the correspondent wondered at it amid the confusion of the sea.

It seemed also very attractive; but the correspondent knew that it was a long journey, and he paddled leisurely. The piece of life preserver lay under him, and sometimes he whirled down the incline of a wave as if he were on a hand-sled.

But finally he arrived at a place in the sea where travel was beset with difficulty. He did not pause swimming to inquire what manner of current had caught him, but there his progress ceased. The shore was set before him like a bit of scenery on a stage, and he looked at it and understood with his eyes each detail of it.

As the cook passed, much farther to the left, the captain was calling to him. "Turn over on your back, cook! Turn over on your back and use the oar."

"All right, sir." The cook turned on his back, and, paddling with an oar, went ahead as if he were a canoe.

Presently the boat also passed to the left of the correspondent, with the captain clinging with one hand to the keel. He would have appeared like a man raising himself to look over a board fence if it were not for the extraordinary gymnastics of the boat. The correspondent marvelled that the captain could still hold to it.

They passed on nearer to shore—the oiler, the cook, the captain—and following them went the water jar, bouncing gaily over the seas.

The correspondent remained in the grip of this strange new enemy, a current. The shore, with its white slope of sand and its green bluff topped with little silent cottages, was spread like a picture before him.

It was very near to him then, but he was impressed as one who, in a gallery, looks at a scene from Brittany or Algiers.

He thought: "I am going to drown? Can it be possible? Can it be possible? Can it be possible?" Perhaps an individual must consider his own death to be the final phenomenon of nature.

But later a wave perhaps whirled him out of this small deadly current, for he found suddenly that he could again make progress toward the shore. Later still he was aware that the captain, clinging with one hand to the keel of the dinghy, had his face turned away from the shore and toward him, and was calling his name. "Come to the boat! Come to the boat!"

In his struggle to reach the captain and the boat, he reflected that when one gets properly wearied drowning must really be a comfortable arrangement—a cessation of hostilities accompanied by a large degree of relief; and he was glad of it, for the main thing in his mind for some moments had been horror of the temporary agony; he did not wish to be hurt.

Presently he saw a man running along the shore. He was undressing with most remarkable speed. Coat, trousers, shirt, everything flew magically off him.

"Come to the boat!" called the captain.

"All right, Captain." As the correspondent paddled, he saw the captain let himself down to bottom and leave the boat. Then the correspondent performed his one little marvel of the voyage. A large wave caught him and flung him with ease and supreme speed completely over the boat and far beyond it. It struck him even then as an event in gymnastics and a true miracle of the sea. An overturned boat in the surf is not a plaything to a swimming man.

The correspondent arrived in water that reached only to his waist, but his condition did not enable him to stand for more than a moment. Each wave knocked him into a heap, and the undertow pulled at him.

Then he saw the man who had been running and undressing, and undressing and running, come bounding into the water. He dragged ashore the cook, and then waded toward the captain; but the captain waved him away and sent him to the correspondent. He was naked—naked as a tree in winter; but a halo was about his head, and he shone like a saint. He gave a strong pull, and a long drag, and a bully heave at the correspondent's hand. The correspondent, schooled in the minor formulae, said, "Thanks, old man." But suddenly the man cried, "What's that?" He pointed a swift finger. The correspondent said, "Go."

In the shallows, face downward, lay the oiler. His forehead touched sand that was periodically, between each wave, clear of the sea.

The correspondent did not know all that transpired afterward. When he achieved safe ground he fell, striking the sand with each particular part of his body. It was as if he had dropped from a roof, but the thud was grateful to him.

It seems that instantly the beach was populated with men with blankets, clothes, and flasks, and women with coffeepots and all the remedies sacred to their minds. The welcome of the land to the men from the sea was warm and generous; but a still and dripping shape was carried slowly up the beach, and the land's welcome for it could only be the different and sinister hospitality of the grave.

When it came night, the white waves paced to and fro in the moonlight, and the wind brought the sound of the great sea's voice to the men on the shore, and they felt that they could then be interpreters.

An early writer, Stephen Crane (1871–1900) worked for his brother's news service in Asbury Park, New Jersey. He became famous for The Red Badge of Courage _(1895). This story from_ The Open Boat and Other Tales _(1898), is the result of Crane being shipwrecked off the coast of Florida._

Strange Tales of the Sea

The Fog

Pierre Loti

In the immense depths surrounding the fisherman, new changes were taking place almost within sight. The majestic unfolding of the infinite—that magnificent spectacle of the morning was ended and now, on the contrary, the horizon seemed to be shrinking, to be closing in upon them. How could the sea have seemed so limitless but a moment before? The horizon was so close at present that it seemed almost to be lacking in space. Tenuous veils floated in the void, some as vague as mist and others more clearly outlined and fringed. They fell softly, like fine white muslin, into the great silence below; they fell everywhere until the air beneath them became heavy and oppressive.

It was the first fog of August. In a few moments the shroud became impenetrable and nothing could be seen but the pale mist in which there was a diffused light, and in which even the masts of the ship seemed to disappear.

"Here comes that damned fog again," said the men.

But they knew well that this inevitable companion to the latter part of their fishing expeditions announced at the same time the end of the Iceland season and their return to Brittany.

Their beards were covered with

brilliant little drops and their tanned skins glistened. They appeared phantom-like when seen from opposite ends of the boat, while, on the contrary, objects close at hand stood out crudely under that dull white light. One was careful not to breathe through the mouth, lest a sensation of cold and dampness penetrate the lungs.

Nevertheless, fishing went on as usual and the lines were being drawn up more and more briskly. Every second one heard a sharp slapping sound like the crack of a whip as the fish were thrown on deck, where they lay madly struggling and flapping their tails against the wooden planks. In their struggles the whole place became spattered with seawater and fine silvery scales. Sometimes, in his haste to slit open their bellies, the sailor cut his own fingers, and his red blood mingled with the brine.

The fog lasted ten days. But, as the fishing continued, their constant activity prevented them from becoming bored. At regular intervals one of the sailors would blow into a horn which emitted a sound like the roar of a wild beast. When a distant sound came in answer to their call, they had to be on their guard. If the call came nearer, all ears were bent in the direction of the unknown neighbor whom they would probably never see, but whose presence remained nevertheless a menace.

They made all sorts of conjectures as to which vessel it might be and, in their desire to see it, their eyes made every effort to pierce the impalpable white curtains hanging in the air.

As the boats drifted apart, the sound of the horn became gradually fainter until it died away in the distance, and then all was silent once more on this infinite expanse where they remained alone amid the motionless vapor.

One morning at about three o'clock, while they were calmly dreaming beneath their shroud of fog, they suddenly heard the sound of voices which seemed strangely unfamiliar. Those on deck looked at one another with questioning glances.

"Who spoke there?"

No, it had not come from the men.

As a matter of fact the voices had seemed to come from the outer regions. The sailor in charge of the foghorn, which he had neglected for some time, rushed to sound the alarm.

This in itself was enough to make them shiver, but what is more, an apparition seemed to have been evoked by the vibrant sound of that horn for suddenly a huge menacing gray object rose unexpectedly before them. It seemed to have come out of nowhere, very much like those phantasmagorias which are created by a play of lights on a screen. It had masts, sails, rigging and every other semblance of a ship. Other men appeared quite close to them, almost within their reach; they were leaning over the railing, a look of amazement and terror in their eyes. . . .

The *Marie's* crew made a wild dash for oars, beams, hooks—anything long and solid that they could lay their hands on—and pointing towards the strange craft, pushed with all their might to keep her at a distance. Now the others, equally frightened, also grasped long poles to keep the *Marie* at a distance.

But there was only a slight cracking sound in the rigging and the sails became detached with very little damage done. The calm had almost completely deadened the shock. It had been so slight, in fact, that the other ship seemed not to have been made of solid substance at all, but of something soft and light.

After the first shock of surprise the men began to laugh, for they had recognized one another.

"Ahoy, the *Marie!*"

"Hey there, Gaos, Laumec, Guermeur!"

The apparition was the *Reine-Berthe* and her captain, Larvoer, was from Paimpol. All these sailors came from neighboring villages; that big one there with the black beard and hearty laugh was Kerjegon from Ploudaniel and the others came from either Plounes or Plounerin.

"Why didn't you blow your horn, you band of savages?" asked Captain Larvoer of the *Reine-Berthe.*

"And why didn't you, you band of pirates and sea robbers?"

"Oh, with us it's quite different—we are forbidden to make noise." (He said this in a mysterious way with a strange smile on his face, which made the sailors suspicious and gave them much to think about in the following days.)

Then, as though he had said too much, he amended it by adding jokingly: "That boy over there blew into our horn so hard that it burst." He pointed to a misshapen creature who had the features of a Triton and who seemed to be all neck and chest. There was something terrifying about his grotesque deformed strength.

The sailors chatted while they waited for a breeze that would separate the boats and carry one off more quickly than the other. They stood on the port side of the ship with their oars poised as though they were being besieged and talked of home, of letters recently received from parents and wives.

"My wife tells me," said Kerjegon, "that she has given birth to the little one we were expecting; the next one will make a round dozen for us."

Another one's wife had had twins and a third announced the coming marriage of Jeannie Caroff, well known to them all, to a rich, sickly old man from Plourivo.

They saw each other as through a white film, and their voices also were strangely altered, muffled and as though coming from afar.

While they were talking Yann was scrutinizing one of the fishermen, an elderly little man whom he felt certain he had never met before, but who had greeted him with a "Hello there, Yann," as though they were on intimate terms. He had the irritating ugliness of a monkey and a twinkle of malice in his piercing eyes.

A SCANDINAVIAN BARK LEAVING PORT

"I have been informed," added Larvoer of the *Reine-Berthe*, "of the death of poor old Yvonne Moan's grandson who, as you all know, was serving in the Navy in China. What a pity!"

Upon hearing this all the men of the *Marie* turned to look at Yann, to see if he already knew of this misfortune.

"Yes," he said softly, but in a haughty, indifferent manner, "my father wrote me about it in his last letter." He was annoyed by their curiosity.

Their remarks were exchanged hastily through the fog while the minutes flew quickly by.

"My wife also wrote," continued Larvoer, "that Monsieur Mevel's daughter left the city to live in Ploubazlanec and take care of old Yvonne, her great-aunt. I always knew she was a fine, brave girl despite her grand airs."

Again they turned to look at Yann and his cheeks reddened beneath their tan. These compliments to Gaud ended the conversation with the men on board the *Reine-Berthe*, whom no living soul was ever to see again. Their faces became indistinct as their ship drifted away. Suddenly the crew of the *Marie*, finding no further need to keep them off with their oars, spars, and masts, let the ends of these useless weapons drop heavily onto the surface of the water like huge lifeless limbs, then gathered them in.

The *Reine-Berthe* plunged once more into the thick fog and disappeared like a transparent image which one effaces by merely blowing out the light behind it.

They tried to hail her but received no answer to their cries—only a sort of mocking clamor ending in groans which made them turn to each other in surprise.

The *Reine-Berthe* did not return with the other Icelanders. As the men on board the *Samuel-Azenide* had come across a wreck in the fjord, which was unquestionably part of her keel and taffrail, no one expected her back.

In the month of October the names of all her sailors were inscribed upon black slabs which were then nailed to the walls of the church.

From the day of that apparition (the date of which the men on board the *Marie* remembered only too well), up to the time of their return, the weather had remained calm while, on the contrary, three weeks before a westerly gale had swept away several sailors and wrecked two vessels. They recalled Larvoer's smile and, bringing these facts together, they made many strange conjectures. The face of the sailor who blinked his eyes like a monkey came back more than once to haunt Yann at night, and there were many on board the *Marie* who wondered timorously whether they had not been talking to the dead on that fatal morning.

Born in France and joining the navy early in life, Pierre Loti (1850–1923) achieved the rank of captain by age seventeen. This excerpt is from An Iceland Fisherman *(1886), a novel about life among the Breton fishermen.*

MS Found in a Bottle

Edgar Allan Poe

Qui n'a plus qu'un moment à vivre
N'a plus rien à dissimuler.—Quinault—Atys.

Of my country and of my family I have little to say. Ill usage and length of years have driven me from the one, and estranged me from the other. Hereditary wealth afforded me an education of no common order, and a contemplative turn of mind enabled me to methodize the stores which early study very diligently garnered up. Beyond all things, the study of the German moralists gave me great delight; not from any ill-advised admiration of their eloquent madness, but from the ease with which my habits of rigid thought enabled me to detect their falsities. I have often been reproached with the aridity of my genius; a deficiency of imagination has been imputed to me as a crime; and the Pyrrhonism of my opinions has at all times rendered me notorious. Indeed, a strong relish for physical philosophy has, I fear, tinctured my mind with a very common error of this age—I mean the habit of referring occurrences, even the least susceptible of such reference, to the principles of that science. Upon the whole, no person could be less liable than myself to be led away from the severe precincts of truth by the *ignes fatui* of superstition. I have thought proper to premise thus much, lest the incredible tale I have to tell should be considered rather the raving of a crude imagination, than the positive experience of a mind to which the reveries of fancy have been a dead letter and a nullity.

After many years spent in foreign travel, I sailed in the year 18—, from the port of Batavia, in the rich and populous island of Java, on a voyage to the Archipelago of the Sunda islands. I went as passenger—having no other inducement than a kind of nervous restlessness which haunted me as a fiend.

Our vessel was a beautiful ship of about four hundred tons, copper-fastened, and built at Bombay of Malabar teak. She was freighted with cotton-wool and oil, from the Laccadive islands. We had also on board coir, jaggery, ghee, coconuts, and a few cases of opium. The stowage was clumsily done, and the vessel consequently crank.

We got under way with a mere breath of wind, and for many days stood along the eastern coast of Java, without any other incident to beguile the monotony of our course than the occasional meeting with some of the small grabs of the archipelago to which we were bound.

One evening, leaning over the taffrail, I observed a very singular, isolated cloud, to the NW. It was remarkable, as well as for its color, as from its being the first we had seen since our departure from Batavia. I watched it attentively until sunset, when it spread all at once to the eastward and westward, girting in the horizon with a narrow strip of vapor, and looking like a long line of low beach. My notice was soon afterwards attracted by the dusky-red appearance of the moon, and the peculiar character of the sea. The latter was undergoing a rapid change, and the water seemed more than usually transparent. Although I could distinctly see the bottom, yet, heaving the lead, I found the ship in fifteen fathoms. The air now became intolerably hot, and was loaded with spiral exhalations similar to those arising from heated iron. As night came on, every breath of wind died away, and a more entire calm it is impossible to conceive. The flame of a candle burned upon the poop without the least perceptible motion, and a long hair, held between the finger and thumb, hung without the possibility of detecting a vibration. However, as the captain said he could perceive no indication of danger, and as we were drifting in bodily to shore, he ordered the sails to be furled, and the anchor let go. No watch was set, and the crew, consisting principally of Malays, stretched themselves deliberately upon deck. I went below—not without a full presentiment of evil. Indeed, every appearance warranted me in apprehending a simoom. I told the captain my fears; but he paid no attention to what I said, and left me without deigning to give a reply. My uneasiness, however, prevented me from sleeping, and about midnight I went upon deck. As I placed my foot upon the upper step of the companion-ladder, I was startled by a loud humming noise, like that occasioned by the rapid revolution of a mill wheel, and before I could ascertain its meaning, I found the ship quivering to its center. In the next instant, a wilderness of foam hurled us upon our beam-ends, and, rushing over us fore and aft swept the entire decks from stem to stern.

The extreme fury of the blast proved, in a great measure, the salvation of the ship. Although completely waterlogged, yet, as her masts had gone by the board, she rose, after a minute, heavily from the sea, and, staggering awhile beneath the immense pressure of the tempest, finally righted.

By what miracle I escaped destruction, it is impossible to say. Stunned by the shock of the water, I found myself, upon recovery, jammed in between the stern-post and rudder. With great difficulty I gained my feet, and looking dizzily around, was, at first, struck with the idea of our being among breakers; so terrific, beyond the wildest imagination, was the whirlpool of mountainous and foaming ocean within which we were engulfed. After a while, I heard the voice of an old Swede, who had shipped with us at the moment of our leaving port. I hallooed to him with all my strength, and presently he came reeling aft. We soon discovered that we were the sole survivors of the accident. All on deck, with the exception of ourselves, had been swept overboard; the captain and mates must have perished as they slept, for the cabins were deluged with water. Without assistance, we could expect to do little for the security of the ship, and our exertions were at first paralyzed by the momentary expectation of going down. Our cable had, of course, parted like packthread, at the first breath of the hurricane, or we should have been instantaneously overwhelmed. We scudded with frightful velocity before the sea, and the water made clear breaches over us. The framework of our stern was shattered excessively, and, in almost every respect, we had received considerable injury; but to our extreme joy we found the pumps unchoked, and that we had made no great shifting of our ballast. The main fury of the blast had already blown over, and we apprehended little danger from the violence of the wind; but we looked forward to its total cessation with dismay; well believing, that, in our shattered condition, we should inevitably perish in the tremendous swell which would ensue. But this very just apprehension seemed by no means likely to be soon verified. For five entire days and nights—during which our only subsistence was a small quantity of jaggery, procured with great difficulty from the forecastle—the hulk flew at a rate defying computation, before rapidly succeeding flaws of wind, which, without equalling the first violence of the simoom, were still more terrific than any tempest I had before encountered. Our course for the first four days was, with trifling variations, SE and by S; and we must have run down the coast of New Holland. On the fifth day the cold became extreme, although the wind had hauled round a point more to the northward. The sun arose with a sickly yellow luster, and clambered a very few degrees above the horizon—emitting no decisive light. There were no clouds apparent, yet the wind was upon the increase, and blew with a fitful and unsteady fury.

"OH GOD PRESERVE THE MARINER," A SONG ILLUSTRATION

About noon, as nearly as we could guess, our attention was again arrested by the appearance of the sun. It gave out no light, properly so called, but a dull and sullen glow without reflection, as if all its rays were polarized. Just before sinking within the turgid sea, its central fires suddenly went out, as if hurriedly extinguished by some unaccountable power. It was a dim, silver-like rim, alone, as it rushed down the unfathomable ocean.

We waited in vain for the arrival of the sixth day—that day to me has not arrived—to the Swede, never did arrive. Thenceforward we were enshrouded in pitchy darkness, so that we could not have seen an object at twenty paces from the ship. Eternal night continued to envelop us, all unrelieved by the phosphoric sea-brilliancy to which we had been accustomed in the tropics. We observed too, that, although the tempest continued to rage with unabated violence, there was no longer to be discovered the usual appearance of surf, or foam, which had hitherto attended us. All around were horror, and thick gloom, and a black sweltering desert of ebony. Superstitious terror crept by degrees into the spirit of the old Swede, and my own soul was wrapped up in silent wonder. We neglected all care of the ship, as worse than useless, and securing ourselves, as well as possible, to the stump of the mizzenmast, looked out bitterly into the world of ocean. We had no means of calculating time, nor could we form any guess of our situation. We were, however, well aware of having made farther to the southward than any previous navigators, and felt great amazement at not meeting with the usual impediments of ice. In the meantime every moment threatened to be our last—every mountainous billow hurried to overwhelm us. The swell surpassed anything I had imagined possible, and that we were not instantly buried is a miracle. My companion spoke of the lightness of our cargo, and reminded me of the excellent qualities of our ship; but I could not help feeling the utter hopelessness of hope itself, and prepared myself gloomily for that death which I thought nothing could defend beyond an hour, as, with every knot of the way the ship made, the swelling of the black stupendous seas became more dismally appalling. At times we gasped for breath at an elevation beyond the albatross—at times became dizzy with the velocity of our descent into some watery hell, where the air grew stagnant, and no sound disturbed the slumbers of the kraken.

We were at the bottom of one of the abysses, when a quick scream from my companion broke fearfully upon the night. "See! see!" cried he, shrieking in my ears, "Almighty God! see! see!" As he spoke I became aware of a dull, sullen glare of red light which streamed down the sides of the vast chasm where we lay, and threw a fitful brilliancy upon our deck. Casting my eyes upwards, I beheld a spectacle which froze the current of my blood. At a terrific height directly above us, and upon the very verge of the precipitous descent, hovered a gigantic ship of, perhaps, four thousand tons. Although upreared upon the summit of a wave more than a hundred times her own altitude, her apparent size still exceeded that of any ship of the line or East Indiaman in existence. Her huge hull was of a deep, dingy black, unrelieved by any of the customary carvings of a ship. A single row of brass cannon protruded from her open ports, and dashed from their polished surfaces the fires of innumerable battle-lanterns, which swung to and fro about her rigging. But what mainly inspired us with horror and astonishment, was that she bore up under a press of sail in the very teeth of that supernatural sea, and of that ungovernable hurricane. When we first discovered her, her bows were alone to be seen, as she rose slowly from the dim and horrible gulf beyond her. For a moment of intense terror she paused upon the giddy pinnacle, as if in contemplation of her own sublimity, then trembled and tottered, and—came down.

At this instant, I know not what sudden self-possession came over my spirit. Staggering as far aft as I could, I awaited fearlessly the ruin that was to overwhelm. Our own vessel was at length ceasing from her struggles, and sinking with her head to the sea. The shock of the descending mass struck her, consequently, in that portion of her frame which was already under water, and the inevitable violence, upon the rigging of the stranger.

As I fell, the ship hove in stays, and went about; and to the confusion ensuing I attributed my escape from the notice of the crew. With little difficulty I made my way unperceived to the main hatchway, which was partially open, and soon found an opportunity of secreting myself in the hold. Why I did so I can hardly tell. An indefinite sense of awe, which at first sight of the navigators of the ship had taken hold of my mind, was perhaps the principle of my concealment. I was unwilling to trust myself with a race of people who had offered, to the cursory glance I had taken, so many points of vague novelty, doubt, and apprehension. I therefore thought proper to contrive a hiding place in the hold. This I did by removing a small portion of the shifting-boards, in such a manner as to afford me a convenient retreat between the huge timbers of the ship.

I had scarcely completed my work, when a footstep in the hold forced me to make use of it. A man passed by my place of concealment with a feeble and unsteady gait. I could not see his face, but had an opportunity of observing his general appearance. There was about it an evidence of great age and infirmity. His knees tottered beneath a load of years, and his entire frame quivered under the burthen. He muttered to himself, in a low broken tone, some words of a language which I could not understand and groped in a corner among a pile of singular-looking instruments and decayed charts of navigation. His manner was a wild mixture of the peevishness of second childhood, and the solemn dignity of a God. He at length went on deck, and I saw him no more.

A feeling, for which I have no name, has taken possession of my soul—a sensation which will admit of no analysis, to which the lessons of by-gone times are inadequate, and for which I fear futurity itself will offer me no key. To a mind constituted like my own, the latter consideration is an evil. I shall never—I know that I shall never—be satisfied with regard to the nature of my conceptions. Yet it is not wonderful that these conceptions are indefinite, since they have their origin in sources so utterly novel. A new sense—a new entity is added to my soul.

It is long since I first trod the deck of this terrible ship, and the rays of my destiny are, I think, gathering to a focus. Incomprehensible men! Wrapped up in meditations of a kind which I cannot divine, they pass me by unnoticed. Concealment is utter folly on my part, for the people *will not see*. It was but just now that I passed directly before the eyes of the mate—it was no long while ago that I ventured into the captain's own private cabin, and took thence the materials with which I write, and have written. I shall from time to time continue this journal. It is true that I may not find an opportunity of transmitting it to the world, but I will not fail to make the endeavor. At the last moment I will enclose the MS in a bottle, and cast it within the sea.

An incident has occurred which has given me new room for meditation. Are such things the operation of ungoverned chance? I had ventured upon deck and thrown myself down, without attracting any notice, among a pile of ratlin-stuff and old sails, in the bottom of the yawl. While musing upon the singularity of my fate, I unwittingly daubed with a tar-brush the edges of a neatly folded studding sail which lay near me on a barrel. The studding sail is now bent upon the ship, and the thoughtless touches of the brush are spread out into the word DISCOVERY.

I have made many observations lately upon the structure of the vessel. Although well armed, she is not, I think, a ship of war. Her rigging, build, and general equipment, all negative a supposition of this kind. What she is not, I can easily perceive—what she is I fear it is impossible to say. I know not how it is, but in scrutinizing her strange model and singular cast of spars, her huge size and overgrown suits of canvas, her severely simple bow and antiquated stern, there will occasionally flash across my mind a sensation of familiar things, and there is always mixed up with such indistinct shadows of recollection, an unaccountable memory of old foreign chronicles and ages long ago.

I have been looking at the timbers of the ship. She is built of a material to which I am a stranger. There is a peculiar character about the wood which strikes me as rendering it unfit for the purpose to which it has been applied. I mean its extreme *porousness*, considered independently of the worm-eaten condition which is a consequence of navigation in these seas, and apart from the rottenness attendant upon age. It will appear perhaps an observation somewhat overcurious, but this wood would have every characteristic of Spanish oak, if Spanish oak were distended by any unnatural means.

In reading the above sentence a curious apothegm of an old weather-beaten Dutch navigator comes full upon my recollection. "It is as sure," he was wont to say, when any doubt was entertained of his veracity, "as sure as there is a sea where the ship itself will grow in bulk like the living body of the seaman."

About an hour ago, I made bold to thrust myself among a group of the crew. They paid me no manner of attention, and, although I stood in the very midst of them all, seemed utterly unconscious of my presence. Like the one I had at first seen in the hold, they all bore about them the marks of a hoary old age. Their knees trembled with infirmity; their shoulders were bent double with decrepitude; their shrivelled skins rattled in the wind; their voices were low, tremulous and broken; their eyes glistened with the rheum of years; and their gray hairs streamed terribly in the tempest. Around them, on every part of the deck, lay scattered mathematical instruments of the most quaint and obsolete construction.

I mentioned some time ago the bending of a studding sail. From that period the ship, being thrown dead off the wind, has continued her terrific course due south, with every rag of canvas packed upon her, from her trucks to her lower studding sail booms, and rolling every moment her topgallant yardarms into the most appalling hell of water which it can enter into the mind of man to imagine. I have just left the deck, where I find it impossible to maintain a footing, although the crew seem to experience little inconvenience. It appears to me a miracle of miracles that our enormous bulk is not swallowed up at once and forever. We are surely doomed to hover continually upon the brink of Eternity, without taking a final plunge into the abyss. From billows a thousand times more stupendous than any I have ever seen, we glide away with the facility of the arrowy sea gull; and the colossal waters rear their heads above us like demons of the deep, but like demons confined to simple threats and forbidden to destroy. I am led to attribute these frequent escapes to the only natural cause which can account for such effect. I must suppose the ship to be within the influence of some strong current, or impetuous undertow.

I have seen the captain face to face, and in his own cabin—but, as I expected, he paid me no attention. Although in his appearance there is, to a casual observer, nothing which might bespeak him more or less than man—still a feeling of irrepressible reverence and awe mingled with the sensation of wonder with which I regarded him. In stature he is nearly my own height; that is, about five feet eight inches. He is of a well-knit and compact frame of body, neither robust nor remarkably otherwise. But it is the singularity of the expression which reigns upon the face—it is the intense, the wonderful, the thrilling evidence of old age, so utter, so extreme, which excites within my spirit a sense—a sentiment ineffable. His forehead, although little wrinkled, seems to bear upon it the stamp of a myriad of years. His gray hairs are records of the past, and his grayer eyes are Sybils of the future. The cabin door was thickly strewn with strange, iron-clasped folios, and mouldering instruments of science, and obsolete, long-forgotten charts. His head was bowed down upon his hands, and he pored, with a fiery unquiet eye, over a paper which I took to be a commission, and which at all events, bore the signature of a monarch. He muttered to himself, as did the first seaman whom I saw in the hold, some low peevish syllables of a foreign tongue, and although the speaker was close at my elbow, his voice seemed to reach my ears from the distance of a mile.

The ship and all in it are imbued with the spirit of Eld. The crew glide to and fro like the ghosts of buried centuries; their eyes have an eager and uneasy meaning; and when their fingers fall athwart my path in the wild glare of the battle-lanterns, I feel as I have never felt before, although I have been all my life a dealer in antiquities, and have imbibed the shadows of fallen columns at Balbec, and Tadmor, and Persepolis, until my very soul has become a ruin.

When I look around me I feel ashamed of my former apprehensions. If I trembled at the blast which has hitherto attended us, shall I not stand aghast at a warring of wind and ocean, to convey any idea of which the words tornado and simoom are trivial and ineffective? All in the immediate vicinity of the ship is the blackness of eternal night, and a chaos of foamless water; but, about a league on either side of us, may be seen, indistinctly and at intervals, stupendous ramparts of ice, towering away into the desolate sky, and looking like the walls of the universe.

As I imagined, the ship proves to be in a current; if that appellation can properly be given to a tide which, howling and shrieking by the white ice, thunders on to the southward with a velocity like the headlong dashing of a cataract.

To conceive the horror of my sensations is, I presume, utterly impossible; yet a curiosity to penetrate the mysteries of these awful regions, predominates even over my despair, and will reconcile me to the most hideous aspect of death. It is evident that we are hurrying onwards to some exciting knowledge—some never-to-be-imparted secret, whose attainment is destruction. Perhaps this current leads us to the southern pole itself. It must be confessed that a supposition apparently so wild has every probability in its favor.

The crew pace the deck with unquiet and tremulous step; but there is upon their countenances an expression more of the eagerness of hope than of the apathy of despair.

In the meantime the wind is still in our poop, and, as we carry a crowd of canvas, the ship is at times lifted bodily from out the sea—Oh, horror upon horror! the ice opens suddenly to the right, and to the left and we are whirling dizzily, in immense concentric circles, round and round the borders of a gigantic amphitheater, the summit of whose walls is lost in the darkness and the distance. But little time will be left me to ponder upon my destiny—the circles rapidly grow small—we are plunging madly within the grasp of the whirlpool—and amid a roaring, and bellowing, and thundering of ocean and of tempest, the ship is quivering, oh God! and—going down.

Born in America, orphaned as a teenager, Edgar Allan Poe (1809–1849) became the ward of a wealthy merchant. Broke and starving after being dismissed from West Point, he was launched into a writing career when this story won a contest, and became a prolific author, editor, and critic. He is famous for Tales of the Grotesque and Arabesque *(1840).*

The Ship That Saw a Ghost

Frank Norris

Very much of this story must remain untold, for the reason that if it were definitely known what business I had aboard the tramp steam-freighter *Glarus*, three hundred miles off the South American coast on a certain summer's day, some few years ago, I would very likely be obliged to answer a great many personal and direct questions put by fussy and impertinent experts in maritime law—who are paid to be inquisitive. Also, I would get "Ally Bazan," Strokher and Hardenberg into trouble.

Suppose on that certain summer's day, you had asked of Lloyds' agency where the *Glarus* was, and what was her destination and cargo. You would have been told that she was twenty days out from Callao, bound north to San Francisco in ballast; that she had been spoken by the bark *Medea* and the steamer *Benevento*; that she was reported to have blown out a cylinder head, but being manageable was proceeding on her way under sail.

That is what Lloyds' would have answered.

If you know something of the ways of ships and what is expected of them, you will understand that the *Glarus*, to be some half a dozen hundred miles south of where Lloyds' would have her, and to be still going south, under full steam, was a scandal that would

have made her brothers and sisters ostracize her finally and forever.

And that is curious, too. Humans may indulge in vagaries innumerable and may go far afield in the way of lying; but a ship may not so much as quibble without suspicion. The least lapse of "regularity," the least difficulty in squaring performance with intuition, and behold she is on the black list and her captain, owners, officers, agents and consignors, and even supercargoes, are asked to explain.

And the *Glarus* was already on the black list. From the beginning her stars had been malign. As the *Breda*, she had first lost her reputation, seduced into a filibustering escapade down the South American coast, where in the end a plainclothes United States detective—that is to say, a revenue cutter—arrested her off Buenos Aires and brought her home, a prodigal daughter, besmirched and disgraced.

After that she was in some dreadful blackbirding business in a far quarter of the South Pacific; and after that—her name changed finally to the *Glarus*—poached seals for a syndicate of Dutchmen who lived in Tacoma, and who afterward built a clubhouse out of what she earned.

And after that we got her.

We got her, I say, through Ryder's South Pacific Exploitation Company. The "President" had picked out a lovely little deal for Hardenberg, Strokher and Ally Bazan (the Three Black Crows), which he swore would make them "independent rich" the rest of their respective lives. It is a promising deal (B. 300 it is on Ryder's map), and if you want to know more about it you may write to ask Ryder what B. 300 is. If he chooses to tell you, that is his affair.

For B. 300—let us confess it—is, as Hardenberg puts it, as crooked as a dog's hind leg. It is as risky as barratry. If you pull it off you may—after paying Ryder his share—divide sixty-five, or possibly sixty-seven, thousand dollars between you and your associates. If you fail, and you are perilously like to fail, you will be sure to have a man or two of your companions shot, maybe yourself obliged to pistol certain people, and in the end fetch up at Tahiti, prisoner in a French patrol boat.

Observe that B.300 is spoken of as still open. It is so, for the reason that the Three Black Crows did not pull it off. It still stands marked up in red ink on the map that hangs over Ryder's desk in the San Francisco office; and any one can have a chance at it who will meet Cyrus Ryder's terms. Only he can't get the *Glarus* for the attempt.

For the trip to the island after B. 300 was the last occasion on which the *Glarus* will smell blue water or taste the trades. She will never clear again. She is lumber.

And yet the *Glarus* on this very blessed day of 1902 is riding to her buoys off Sausalito in San Francisco Bay, complete in every detail (bar a broken propeller shaft); not a rope missing, not a screw loose, not a plank started—a perfectly equipped steam-freighter.

But you may go along the "Front" in San Francisco from Fisherman's Wharf to the China steamships' docks and shake your dollars under the seamen's noses, and if you so much as whisper *Glarus* they will edge suddenly off and look at you with scared suspicion, and then, as like as not, walk away without another word. No pilot will take the *Glarus* out; no captain will navigate her; no stoker will feed her fires; no sailor will walk her decks. The *Glarus* is suspect. She has seen a ghost.

It happened on our voyage to the island after this same B. 300. We had stood well off from shore for day after day, and Hardenberg had shaped our course so far from the track of navigation that since the *Benevento* had hulled down and vanished over the horizon no stitch of canvas nor smudge of smoke had we seen. We had passed the equator long since, and would fetch a long circuit to the southard, and bear up against the island by a circuitous route. This to avoid being spoken. It was tremendously essential that the *Glarus* should not be spoken.

I suppose, no doubt, that it was the knowledge of our isolation that impressed me with the dreadful remoteness of our position. Certainly the sea in itself looks no different at a thousand than at a hundred miles from shore. But as day after day I came out on deck at noon, after ascertaining our position on the chart (a mere pinpoint in a reach of empty paper), the sight of the ocean weighed down upon me with an infinitely great awesomeness—and I was no new hand to the high seas even then.

But at such times the *Glarus* seemed to me to be threading a loneliness beyond all worlds and beyond all conception desolate. Even in more populous waters, when no sail notches the line of the horizon, the propinquity of one's kind is nevertheless a thing understood, and to an unappreciated degree comforting. Here, however, I knew we were out, far out in the desert. Never a keel for years upon years before us had parted these waters; never a sail had bellied to these winds. Perfunctorily, day in and day out we turned our eyes through long habit toward the horizon. But we knew, before the look, that the searching would be bootless. Forever and forever, under the pitiless sun and cold blue sky stretched the indigo of the ocean floor. The ether between the planets can be no less empty, no less void.

I never, till that moment, could have so much as conceived the imagination of such loneliness, such utter stagnant abomination of desolation. In an open boat, bereft of comrades, I should have gone mad in thirty minutes.

I remember to have approximated the impression of such empty immensity only once before, in my younger days, when I lay on my back on a treeless, bushless mountainside and stared up into the sky for the better part of an hour.

You probably know the trick. If you do not, you must understand that it you look up at the blue long enough, the flatness of the thing begins little by little to expand, to give here and there; and the eye travels on and on and up and up, till at length (well for you that it lasts but the fraction of a second) you all at once see space. You generally stop there and cry out, and—your hands over your eyes—are only too glad to grovel close to the good old solid earth again. Just as I, so often on short voyage, was glad to wrench my eyes away from that horrid vacancy, to fasten them upon our sailless masts and stack, or to lay my grip upon the sooty smudged taffrail of the only thing that stood between me and the Outer Dark.

For we had come at last to that region of the Great Seas where no ship goes, the silent sea of Coleridge and the Ancient One, the unplumbed, untracked, uncharted dreadfulness, primordial, hushed, and we were as much alone as a grain of stardust whirling in the empty space beyond Uranus and the ken of the greater telescopes.

So the *Glarus* plodded and churned her way onward. Every day and all day the same pale-blue sky and the unwinking sun bent over that moving speck. Every day and all day the same black-blue water-world, untouched by any known wind, smooth as a slab of syenite, colorful as an opal, stretched out and around and beyond and before and behind us, forever, illimitable, empty. Every day the smoke of our fires veiled the streaked whiteness of our wake. Every day Hardenberg (our skipper) at noon pricked a pinhole in the chart that hung in the wheelhouse, and that showed we were so much farther into the wilderness. Every day the world of men, of civilization, of newspapers, policemen and street railways receded, and we steamed on alone, lost and forgotten in that silent sea.

"Jolly lot o' room to turn raound in," observed Ally Bazan, the colonial, "withaout steppin' on y'r neighbour's toes."

"We're clean, clean out o' the track o' navigation," Hardenberg told him. "An' a blessed good thing for us, too. Nobody ever comes down into these waters. Ye couldn't pick no course here. Everything leads to nowhere."

"Might as well be in a bally balloon," said Strokher.

I shall not tell of the nature of the venture on which the *Glarus* was bound, further than to say it was not legitimate. It had to do with an ill thing done more than two centuries ago. There was money in the venture, but it was not to be gained by a violation of metes and bounds which are better left intact.

The island toward which we were heading is associated in the minds of men with a horror. A ship had called there once, two hundred years in advance of the *Glarus*—a ship not much unlike the crank high-prowed caravel of Hudson, and her company had landed, and having accomplished the evil they had set out to do, made shift to sail away. And then, just after the palms of the island had sunk from sight below the water's edge, the unspeakable had happened. The Death that was not Death had arisen from out the sea and stood before the ship, and over it, and the blight of the thing lay along the decks like mould, and the ship sweated in the terror of that which is yet without a name.

Twenty men died in the first week, all but six in the second. These six, with the shadow of insanity upon them, made out to launch a boat, returned to the island and died there, after leaving a record of what had happened.

The six left the ship exactly as she was, sails all set, lanterns all lit—left her in the shadow of the Death that was not Death. She stood there, becalmed, and watched them go. She was never heard of again.

Or was she—well, that's as may be. But the main point of the whole affair, to my notion, has always been this. The ship was the last friend of those six poor wretches who made back for the island with their poor chests of plunder. She was their guardian, as it were, would have defended and befriended them to the last; and also we, the Three Black Crows and myself, had no right under heaven, nor before the law of men, to come prying and peeping into this business—into this affair of the dead and buried past. There was sacrilege in it. We were no better than body snatchers.

When I heard the others complaining of the loneliness of our surroundings, I said nothing at first. I was no sailor man, and I was on board only by tolerance. But I looked again at the maddening sameness of the horizon—the same vacant, void horizon that we had seen now for sixteen days on end, and felt in my wits and in my nerves that same formless rebellion and protest such as comes when the same note is reiterated over and over again.

A PASSENGER LAUNCH CHURNS PAST A MOORED FREIGHTER AND SAILING SHIP

It may seem a little thing that the mere fact of meeting with no other ship should have ground down the edge of the spirit. But let the incredulous—bound upon such a hazard as ours—sail straight into nothingness for sixteen days on end, seeing nothing but the sun, hearing nothing but the thresh of his own screw, and then put the question.

And yet, of all things, we desired no company. Stealth was our one great aim. But I think there were moments—toward the last—when the Three Crows would have welcomed even a cruiser.

Besides, there was more cause for depression, after all, than mere isolation.

On the seventh day Hardenberg and I were forward by the cathead, adjusting the grain with some half-formed intent of spearing the porpoises that of late had begun to appear under our bows, and Hardenberg had been computing the number of days we were yet to run.

"We are some five hundred odd miles off that island by now," he said, "and she's doing her thirteen knots handsome. All's well so far—but do you know, I'd just as soon raise that point o' land as soon as convenient."

"How so?" said I, bending on the line. "Expect some weather?"

"Mr. Dixon," said he, giving me curious glance, "the sea is a queer proposition, put it any ways. I've been a seafarin' man since I was big as a minute and I know the sea, and what's more, the Feel o' the sea. Now, look out yonder. Nothin', hey? Nothin' but the same ol' skyline we've watched all the way out. The glass is as steady as a steeple, and this ol' hooker, I reckon, is as sound as the day she went off the ways. But just the same if I were to home now, a-foolin' about Gloucester way in my little dough-dish—d'ye know what? I'd put into port. I sure would. Because why? Because I got the Feel o' the Sea, Mr. Dixon. I got the Feel o' the Sea."

I had heard old skippers say something of this before, and I cited to Hardenberg the experience of a skipper captain I once knew who had turned turtle in a calm sea off Trincomalee. I asked him what this Feel of the Sea was warning him against just now (for on the high sea any premonition is a premonition of evil, not of good). But he was not explicit.

"I don't know," he answered moodily, and as if in great perplexity, coiling the rope as he spoke. "I don't know. There's some blame thing or other close to us, I'll bet a hat. I don't know the name of it, but there's a big bird in the air, just out of sight som'eres, and," he

125

suddenly exclaimed, smacking his knee and leaning forward, "I—don't—like—it—one—dam'—bit."

The same thing came up in our talk in the cabin that night, after the dinner was taken off and we settled down to tobacco. Only, at this time, Hardenberg was on duty on the bridge. It was Ally Bazan who spoke instead.

"Seems to me," he hazarded, "as haow they's somethin' or other a-goin' to bump up pretty blyme soon. I shouldn't be surprised, naow, y'know, if we piled her up on some bally uncharted reef along o' tonight and went strite daown afore we'd had a bloomin' charnce to s'y 'So long, gen'lemen all.'"

He laughed as he spoke, but when, just at that moment, a pan clattered in the galley, he jumped suddenly with an oath, and looked hard about the cabin.

Then Strokher confessed to a sense of distress also. He'd been having it since day before yesterday, it seemed.

"And I put it to you the glass is lovely," he said, "so it's no blow. I guess," he continued, "we're all a bit seedy and ship-sore."

And whether or not this talk worked upon my own nerves, or whether in very truth the Feel of the Sea had found me also, I do not know; but I do know that after dinner that night, just before going to bed, a queer sense of apprehension came upon me, and that when I had come to my stateroom, after my turn upon deck, I became furiously angry with nobody in particular, because I could not at once find the matches. But here was a difference. The other men had been merely vaguely uncomfortable.

I could put a name to my uneasiness. I felt that we were being watched.

It was a strange ship's company we made after that. I speak only of the Crows and myself. We carried a scant crew of stokers, and there was also a chief engineer. But we saw so little of him that he did not count. The Crows and I gloomed on the quarterdeck from dawn to dark, silent, irritable, working upon each other's nerves till the creak of a block would make a man jump like cold steel laid to his flesh. We quarreled over absolute nothings, glowered at each other for half a word, and each one of us, at different times, was at some pains to declare that never in the course

of his career had he been associated with such a disagreeable trio of brutes. Yet we were always together, and sought each other's company with painful insistence.

Only once were we all agreed, and that was when the cook, a Chinaman, spoiled a certain batch of biscuits. Unanimously we fell foul of the creature with so much vociferation as fishwives till he fled the cabin in actual fear of mishandling, leaving us suddenly seized with noisy hilarity—for the first time in a week. Hardenberg proposed a round of drinks from our single remaining case of beer. We stood up and formed an Elk's chain and then drained our glasses to each other's health with profound seriousness.

That same evening, I remember, we all sat on the quarterdeck till late and—oddly enough—related each one his life's history up to date; and then went down to the cabin for a game of euchre before turning in.

We had left Strokher on the bridge—it was his watch—and had forgotten all about him in the interest of the game, when—I suppose it was about one in the morning—I heard him whistle long and shrill. I laid down my cards and said, "Hark!"

In the silence that followed we heard at first only the muted lope of our engines, the cadenced snorting of the exhaust, and the ticking of Hardenberg's big watch in his waistcoat that he had hung by the armhole to the back of his chair. Then from the bridge, above our deck, prolonged, intoned—a wailing cry in the night—came Strokher's voice:

"Sail oh-h-h."

And the cards fell from our hands, and, like men turned to stone, we sat looking at each other across the soiled red cloth for what seemed an immeasurably long minute.

Then stumbling and swearing, in a hysteria of hurry we gained the deck.

There was a moon, very low and reddish, but no wind. The sea beyond the taffrail was as smooth as lava, and so still that the swells from the cutwater of the *Glarus* did not break as they rolled away from the bows.

I remember that I stood staring and blinking at the empty ocean—where the moonlight lay like a painted stripe reaching to the horizon—stupid and frowning, till Hardenberg, who had gone on ahead, cried:

"Not here—on the bridge!"

We joined Strokher, and as I came up the others were asking, "Where? Where?"

And there, before he had pointed, I saw—we all of us saw—And I heard Hardenberg's teeth come together like a spring trap, while Ally Bazan ducked as though to a blow, muttering:

"Gord 'a' mercy, what nyme do ye put to a ship like that?"

And after that no one spoke for a long minute, and we stood there, moveless black shadows, huddled together for the sake of the blessed elbow touch that means so incalculably much, looking off over our port quarter.

For the ship that we saw there—oh, she was not a half mile distant—was unlike any ship known to present day construction.

She was short, and high-pooped, and her stern, which was turned a little toward us, we could see, was set with curious windows, not unlike a house. And on either side of this stern were two great iron cressets such as once were used to burn signal fires in. She had three masts with mighty yards swung 'thwart ship, but bare of all sails save a few rotting streamers. Here and there about her a tangled mass of rigging drooped and sagged.

And there she lay, in the red eye of the setting moon, in that solitary ocean, shadowy, antique, forlorn, a thing the most abandoned, the most sinister I ever remember to have seen.

Then Strokher began to explain volubly and with many repetitions.

"A derelict, of course. I was asleep; yes, I was asleep. Gross neglect of duty. I say I was asleep—on watch. And we worked up to her. When I woke, why— you see, when I woke, there she was," he gave a weak little laugh, "and—and now, why, there she is, you see. I turned around and saw her sudden like—when I woke up, that is."

He laughed again, and as he laughed the engines far below our feet gave a sudden hiccough. Something crashed and struck the ship's sides till we lurched as we stood. There was a shriek of steam, a shout—and then silence.

The noise of the machinery ceased; the *Glarus* slid through the still water, moving only by her own decreasing momentum.

Hardenberg sang, "Stand by!" and called down the tube to the engine room.

"What's up?"

I was standing close enough to him to hear the answer in a small, faint voice:

"Shaft gone, sir."

"Broke?"

"Yes, sir."

Hardenberg faced about.

"Come below. We must talk." I do not think any of us cast a glance at the other ship again. Certainly I kept my eyes away from her. But as we started down the companionway I laid my hand on Strokher's shoulder. The rest were ahead. I looked him straight between the eyes as I asked:

"Were you asleep? Is that why you saw her so suddenly?"

It is now five years since I asked the question. I am still waiting for Strokher's answer.

Well, our shaft was broken. That was flat. We went down into the engine room and saw the jagged fracture that was the symbol of our broken hopes. And in the course of the next five minutes' conversation with the chief we found that, as we had not provided against such a contingency, there was to be no mending of it. We said nothing about the mishap coinciding with the appearance of the other ship. But I know we did not consider the break with any degree of surprise after a few moments.

We came up from the engine room and sat down to the cabin table.

"Now what?" said Hardenberg, by way of beginning.

Nobody answered at first.

It was by now three in the morning. I recall it all perfectly. The ports opposite where I sat were open and I could see. The moon was all but full set. The dawn was coming up with a copper murkiness over the edge of the world. All the stars were yet out. The sea, for all the red moon and copper dawn, was gray, and there, less than half a mile away, still lay our consort. I could see her through the portholes with each slow careening of the *Glarus*.

"I vote for the island," cried Ally Bazan, "shaft or no shaft. We rigs a bit o' syle, y'know—" and thereat the discussion began.

For upward of two hours it raged, with loud words and shaken forefingers, and great noisy bangings of the table, and how it would have ended I do not know, but at last—it was then maybe five in the morning—the lookout passed word down to the cabin:

"Will you come on deck, gentlemen?" It was the mate who spoke, and the man was shaken—I could see that—to the very vitals of him. We started and stared at one another, and I watched little Ally Bazan go slowly white to the lips. And even then no word of the ship, except as it might be this from Hardenberg:

"What is it? Good God Almighty, I'm no coward, but this thing is getting one too many for me."

Then without further speech he went on deck.

The air was cool. The sun was not yet up. It was that strange, queer midperiod between dark and dawn, when the night is over and the day not yet come, just the gray that is neither light nor dark, the dim dead blink as of the refracted light from extinct worlds.

We stood at the rail. We did not speak; we stood watching. It was so still that the drip of steam from some loosened pipe far below was plainly audible, and it sounded in that lifeless, silent grayness like—God knows what—a death tick.

"You see," said the mate, speakin' just above a whisper, "there's no mistake about it. She is moving—this way."

"Oh, a current, of course," Strokher tried to say cheerfully, "sets her toward us."

Would the morning never come?

Ally Bazan—his parents were Catholic—began to mutter to himself.

Then Hardenberg spoke aloud.

"I particularly don't want—that—out—there—to cross our bows. I don't want it to come to that. We must get some sails on her."

"And I put it to you as man to man," said Strokher, "where might be your wind?"

He was right. The *Glarus* floated in absolute calm. On all that slab of ocean nothing moved but the Dead Ship.

She came on slowly; her bows, the high, clumsy bows pointed toward us, the water turning from her forefoot. She came on; she was near at hand. We saw her plainly—saw the rotted planks, the crumbling rigging, the rust-corroded metalwork, the broken rail, the gap-

ing deck, and I could imagine that the clean water broke away from her sides in refluent wavelets as though in recoil from a thing unclean. She made no sound. No single thing stirred aboard the hulk of her—but she moved.

We were helpless. The *Glarus* could stir no boat in any direction; we were chained to the spot. Nobody had thought to put out our lights, and they still burned on through the dawn, strangely out of place in their red-and-green garishness, like maskers surprised by daylight.

And in the silence of that empty ocean, in that queer half-light between dawn and day, at six o'clock, silent as the settling of the dead to the bottomless bottom of the ocean, gray as fog, lonely, blind, soulless, voiceless, the Dead Ship crossed our bows.

I do not know how long after this the Ship disappeared, or what was the time of day when we at last pulled ourselves together. But we came to some sort of decision at last. This was to go on—under sail. We were too close to the island now to turn back for—for a broken shaft.

The afternoon was spent fitting on the sails to her, and when after nightfall the wind at length came up fresh and favorable, I believe we all felt heartened and a deal more hardy—until the last canvas went aloft, and Hardenberg took the wheel.

We had drifted a good deal since the morning, and the bows of the *Glarus* were pointed homeward, but as soon as the breeze blew strong enough to get steerage-way Hardenberg put the wheel over and, as the booms swung across the deck, headed for the island again.

We had not gone on this course half an hour—no, not twenty minutes—before the wind shifted a whole quarter of the compass and took the *Glarus* square in the teeth, so that there was nothing for it but to tack. And then the strangest thing befell.

I will make allowance for the fact that there was no centerboard nor keel to speak of to the *Glarus*. I will admit that the sails upon a nine-hundred-ton freighter are not calculated to speed her, nor steady her. I will even admit the possibility of a current that set from the island toward us. All this may be true, yet the *Glarus* should have advanced. We should have made a wake.

And instead of this, our stolid, steady, trusty old boat was—what shall I say?

128

I will say that no man may thoroughly understand a ship—after all. I will say that new ships are cranky and unsteady; that old and seasoned ships have their little crotchets, their little fussinesses that their skippers must learn and humor if they are to get anything out of them; that even the best ships may sulk at times, shirk their work, grow unstable, perverse, and refuse to answer helm and handling. And I will say that some ships that for years have sailed blue water as soberly and as docilely as a streetcar horse has plodded the treadmill of the 'tween-tracks, have been known to balk, as stubbornly and as conclusively as any old Bay Billy that ever wore a bell. I know this has happened, because I have seen it. I saw, for instance, the *Glarus* do it.

Quite literally and truly we could do nothing with her. We will say, if you like, that that great jar and wrench when the shaft gave way shook her and crippled her. It is true, however, that whatever the cause may have been, we could not force her toward the island. Of course, we all said "current"; but why didn't the log line trail?

For three days and three nights we tried it. And the *Glarus* heaved and plunged and shook herself just as you have seen a horse plunge and rear when his rider tries to force him at the steamroller.

I tell you I could feel the fabric of her tremble and shudder from bow to sternpost, as though she were in a storm; I tell you she fell off from the wind, and broad-on drifted back from her course till the sensation of her shrinking was as plain as her own staring lights and a thing pitiful to see.

We roweled her, and we crowded sail upon her, and we coaxed and bullied and humored her, till the Three Crows, their fortune only a plain sail two days ahead, raved and swore like insensate brutes, or shall we say like mahouts trying to drive their stricken elephant upon the tiger—and all to no purpose. "Damn the damned current and the damned luck and the damned shaft and all." Hardenberg would exclaim, as from the wheel he would catch the *Glarus* falling off. "Go on, you old hooker—you tub of junk! My God, you'd think she was scared!"

Perhaps the *Glarus* was scared, perhaps not; that point is debatable. But it was beyond doubt of debate that Hardenberg was scared.

A ship that will not obey is only one degree less terrible than a mutinous crew. And we were in a fair way to have both. The stokers, whom we had impressed into duty as AB's, were of course superstitious; and they knew how the *Glarus* was acting, and it was only a question of time before they got out of hand.

That was the end. We held a final conference in the cabin and decided that there was no help for it—we must turn back.

And back we accordingly turned, and at once the wind followed us, and the "current" helped us, and the water churned under the forefoot of the *Glarus*, and the wake whitened under her stern, and the log line ran out from the trail and strained back as the ship worked homeward.

We had never a mishap from the time we finally swung her about; and, considering the circumstances, the voyage back to San Francisco was propitious.

But an incident happened just after we had started back. We were perhaps some five miles on the homeward track. It was early evening and Strokher had the watch. At about seven o'clock he called me up on the bridge.

"See her?" he said.

And there, far behind us, in the shadow of the twilight, loomed the other ship again, desolate, lonely beyond words. We were leaving her rapidly astern. Strokher and I stood looking at her till she dwindled to a dot. Then Strokher said:

"She's on post again."

And when months afterward we limped into the Golden Gate and cast anchor off the "Front" our crew went ashore as soon as discharged, and in half a dozen hours the legend was in every sailors' boardinghouse and in every seaman's dive, from Barbary Coast to Black Tom's.

It is still there, and that is why no pilot will take the *Glarus* out, no captain will navigate her, no stoker feed her fires, no sailor walk her decks. The *Glarus* is suspect. She will never smell blue water again, nor taste the trades. She has seen a ghost.

Born in Chicago, Frank Norris (1870–1902) pursued many interests but finally began writing and worked as assistant to the editor of the San Francisco Wave *in 1896. He became well-known for his novel* The Octopus *(1901).*

Reflections on the Sea

The Sound of the Sea

Henry Beston

The three great sounds in nature are the sound of rain, the sound of wind in a primeval wood, and the sound of outer ocean on a beach. I have heard them all, and of the three elemental voices, that of ocean is the most awesome, beautiful, and varied. For it is a mistake to talk of the monotone of ocean or of the monotonous nature of its sound. The sea has many voices. Listen to the surf, really lend it your ears, and you will hear in it a world of sounds: hollow boomings and heavy roarings, great watery tumblings and tramplings, long hissing seethes, sharp, rifle-shot reports, splashes, whispers, the grinding undertone of stones, and sometimes vocal sounds that might be the half-heard talk of people in the sea. And not only is the great sound varied in the manner of its making, it is also constantly changing its tempo, its pitch, its accent, and its rhythm, being now loud and thundering, now almost placid, now furious, now grave and solemn-slow, now a simple measure, now a rhythm monstrous with a sense of purpose and elemental will.

Every mood of the wind, every change in the day's weather, every phase of the tide—all these have subtle sea musics all their own. Surf of the ebb, for instance, is one music, surf of the flood another, the change in the two musics being most clearly marked during the first hour of a rising tide. With the renewal of the tidal energy, the sound of the surf grows louder, the fury of battle returns to it as it turns again on the land, and beat and sound change with the renewal of the war.

Sound of surf in these autumnal dunes—the continuousness of it, sound of endless charging, endless incoming and gathering, endless fulfillment and dissolution, endless fecundity, and endless death. I have been trying to study out the mechanics of that mighty resonance. The dominant note is the great spilling crash made by each arriving wave. It may be hollow and booming, it may be heavy and churning, it may be a tumbling roar. The second fundamental sound is the wild seething cataract roar of the wave's dissolution and the rush of its foaming waters up the beach—this second sound *diminuendo*. The third fundamental sound is the endless dissolving hiss of the inmost slides of foam. The first two sounds reach the ear as a unisonance—the booming impact of the tons of water and the wild roar of the up-rush blending—and this mingled sound dissolves into the foam-bubble hissing of the third. Above the tumult, like birds, fly wisps of watery noise, splashes and counter splashes, whispers, seethings, slaps, and chucklings. An overtone sound of other breakers, mingled with a general rumbling, fells earth and sea and air.

A naturalist, Henry Beston (1888–1968) lived in a tiny house on the far outer reaches of Cape Cod, Massachusetts, during one year to observe and write about the seasons on the seashore. This selection is from The Outermost House *(1928).*

132

Where Lies the Land to Which the Ship Would Go?

Arthur Hugh Clough

Where lies the land to which the ship would go?
Far, far ahead, is all her seamen know.
And where the land she travels from? Away,
Far, far behind, is all that they can say.

On sunny noons upon the deck's smooth face,
Linked arm in arm, how pleasant here to pace;
Or, o'er the stern reclining, watch below
The foaming wake far widening as we go.

On stormy nights when wild northwesters rave,
how proud a thing to fight with wind and wave!
The dripping sailor on the reeling mast
Exults to bear, and scorns to wish it past.

Where lies the land to which the ship would go?
Far, far ahead, is all her seamen know.
And where the land she travels from? Away,
Far, far behind is all that they can say.

The Sound of the Sea

Henry Wadsworth Longfellow

The sea awoke at midnight from its sleep,
 And round the pebbly beaches far and wide
 I heard the first wave of the rising tide
 Rush onward with uninterrupted sweep;
A voice out of the silence of the deep,
 A sound mysteriously multiplied
 As of a cataract from the mountain's side,
 Or roar of winds upon a wooded steep.
So comes to us at times, from the unknown
 And inaccessible solitudes of being,
 The rushing of the sea-tides of the soul;
And inspirations, that we deem our own,
 Are some divine foreshadowing and foreseeing
 Of things beyond our reason or control.

By the Sea

Christina Rossetti

Why does the sea moan evermore?
    Shut out from heaven it makes its moan,
It frets against the boundary shore:
    All earth's full rivers cannot fill
    The sea, that drinking thirsteth still.

Sheer miracles of loveliness
    Lie hid in its unlooked-on bed:
Anemones, salt, passionless,
    Blow flower-like—just enough alive
    To blow and multiply and thrive.

Shells quaint with curve or spot or spike,
    Encrusted live things argus-eyed,
All fair alike yet all unlike,
    Are born without a pang, and die
    Without a pang, and so pass by.

The Shell

James Stephens

And then I pressed the shell
Close to my ear
And listened well,
And straightway like a bell
Came low and clear
The slow, sad murmur of the distant seas,
Whipped by an icy breeze
Upon a shore
Windswept and desolate.
It was a sunless strand that never bore
The footprint of a man,
Nor felt the weight
Since time began
Of any human quality or stir
Save what the dreary winds and waves incur.

And in the hush of waters was the sound
Of pebbles rolling round,
For ever rolling with a hollow sound.
And bubbling seaweeds as the waters go
Swish to and fro
Their long, cold tentacles of slimy gray.
There was no day,
Nor felt the weight
Setting the stars alight
To wonder at the moon:
Was twilight only and the frightened croon,
Smitten to whimpers, of the dreary wind
And waves that journeyed blind—
And then I loosed my ear . . . O, it was sweet
To hear a cart go jolting down the street.

Dover Beach

Matthew Arnold

The sea is calm tonight.
The tide is full, the moon lies fair
Upon the straits; on the French coast the light
Gleams and is gone; the cliffs of England stand,
Glimmering and vast, out in the tranquil bay.
Come to the window, sweet is the night air!

Only, from the long line of spray
Where the sea meets the moon-blanch'd land,
Listen! you hear the grating roar
Of pebbles which the waves draw back, and fling,
At their return, up the high strand,
Begin, and cease, and then again begin,
With tremulous cadence slow, and bring
The eternal note of sadness in.

Sophocles long ago
Heard it on the Aegean, and it brought
Into his mind the turbid ebb and flow
Of human misery; we
Find also in the sound a thought,
Hearing it by this distant northern sea.

The Sea of Faith
Was once, too, at the full, and round earth's shore
Lay like the folds of a bright girdle furl'd.
But now I only hear
Its melancholy, long, withdrawing roar,
Retreating, to the breath
Of the night-wind, down the vast edges drear
And naked shingles of the world.

Ah, love, let us be true
To one another! for the world, which seems
To lie before us like a land of dreams,
So various, so beautiful, so new,
Hath really neither joy, nor love, nor light,
Nor certitude, nor peace, nor help for pain;
And we are here as on a darkling plain
Swept with confused alarms of struggle and flight,
Where ignorant armies clash by night.

Glossary of Sailing Terms

A.B. An able-bodied or experienced seaman.

abaft To the rear of.

abeam Running at right angles to the longitudinal line of a vessel.

aft The back end of a vessel. Behind.

aloft Up in the tops, at the mastheads, or anywhere about the higher yards and rigging.

alow Below.

amidships The middle of a ship, either along her length or across her breadth.

astern Behind a ship.

athwart Across. In navigation, across the line of a ship's course.

aweather On or toward the weather or windward side.

backstay A stay extending from the mastheads to the sides of a ship and slanting aft.

ballast Any weight, not part of the regular cargo or stores, carried by a ship for stability.

barratry A fraudulent breach of duty on the part of a master of a ship or of the mariners, to the injury of the owner of the ship or cargo.

battery A number of cannon positioned along a sailing warship's rail, on two or more decks.

beam One of a number of thick strong timbers stretching across the ship from side to side, supporting the deck and sides, and firmly connected to the frames by strong knees.

Before the mast Expression used to describe a seaman or rating. Derived from the past practice of accommodating common sailors in the forecastle while the officers were accommodated aft.

belay Make a line secure by wrapping it around a cleat or belaying pin.

binnacle A housing for the ship's compass and a lamp.

blackbirding To kidnap for use or sale as laborers.

block A piece of wood with wheels in it, through which a line is pulled and held in place.

bonnet An additional piece of canvas laced to the foot of a jib or lower square sail.

boom A long horizontal spar used to secure the foot of a sail.

bosun or *boatswain* A petty officer on a merchant ship having responsibility for the maintenance of the hull and related equipment.

bow The fore end of a ship or boat.

bowman A boatman or oarsman stationed in the front of a boat.

bowsprit A large spar which runs out from a vessel's bow and to which all the stays of the foremast are secured.

brace A line rove through a block at the end of a ship's yard to swing it and trim the sails to the wind.

brig A two-masted vessel, square-rigged on both masts.

broaches to also *brought by the lee* To veer dangerously so as to lie broadside to the waves.

broadside The whole side of a vessel. In reference to a naval engagement it signifies a simultaneous discharge of all the guns one one side of a warship.

brought by the lee See *broaches to*.

bulkhead A partition which separates one part or cabin of a vessel from another.

bulwark The side of a ship above the upper deck.

bunt The middle of a square sail, more particularly when furled to the yard.

bunting A lightweight, loosely woven fabric used chiefly for flags and signals.

bunt-lines Lines fastened to the foot ropes of the square sail to draw it up to the middle of the yard and facilitate furling.

by the board A mast falling is said to *go by the board*, when it has given way at or near the deck.

cachalot A sperm whale.

camel A device used for raising ships in the water over areas too shallow to pass.

cannonade A heavy, continuous fire of artillery.

capstan A machine for moving or raising heavy weights that consists of a vertical drum, which can be rotated and around which a cable is turned.

carronade A kind of ship's cannon which is shorter than the customary long gun.

cat's-paw A light current of air which touches the surface of the water lightly, while all around is calm, and passes away.

cathead A stong timber near the bow, used for securing the anchor.

chronometer A very accurate timepiece.

clap on To increase power by adding to the number of purchases used or by using more men; also to set more sails.

claw off A term sometimes used to denote the act of tacking to windward in order to get off a lee shore.

clew Either of the lower corners of a square sail; the aft lower corner of a fore and aft sail; or a metal loop attached to the lower corner of a sail.

clew up or *down* To haul a sail up or down by lines through the clews.

close-hauled A vessel going to windward is said to be sailing *close-hauled*, that is, with her sails "trimmed in."

coach or *coach-house* A name which was given to a sort of apartment beneath the poop deck near the stern of a large ship.

coir A kind of cordage made from the fibrous covering of the coconut.

combing sea Large, breaking waves.

companionway or *companion-ladder* A ship's stairway from one deck to another or to the cabins.

copper-fastened A term describing a vessel who's keel, keelson, transoms and other parts below the wales securely bound by copper bolts.

crab-windlass See *windlass*.

crank (short for *crank-sided*) A term applied to a vessel which will not stand up to her canvas, or, in other words, is too apt to be heeled by the pressure of her sails.

cresset An iron vessel or basket used for holding oil, which is mounted as a torch or suspended as a lantern.

cutter A ship's boat for carrying stores or passengers, or a fore-and-aft rigged sailing vessel with a single mast carying a jib, forestaysail, and mainsail.

doldrums Area of low pressure near the equator between the trade winds, having calms and light variable winds alternating with squalls, heavy rains and thunder storms.

down weather See *downwind*.

downwind In the direction that the wind is blowing.

dreadnought A warm garment of thick cloth.

ensign A flag that is flown as the symbol of nationality.

fathom A unit of length equal to six feet.

fill A sail that is properly trimmed to catch the wind is said to be *filled*.

finneskoe Tanned reindeer skin.

fjord A narrow inlet of the sea between cliffs or steep slopes.

flying-jib A sail flown outside the jib on an extension of the jib boom.

fo'c'sle Variation of *forecastle*.

fore-and-aft sail A triangular sail that is rigged parallel to the keel.

forecastle A raised section in the foremost part of a ship's deck, in which the seamen usually slept.

foremast The mast nearest the bow of the ship.

foresail A sail carried on the foreyard of a square-rigged ship that is the lowest sail on the foremast.

forepeak The extreme forward lower compartment or tank used for trimming or storage in a ship.

fore-scuttle See *scuttle*.

forestaysail The triangular, aftermost headsail set on the forestay.

foretop The platform located part way up a ship's foremast.

full-rigged ship A sailing ship of three or more masts with square rig on all masts.

furl To wrap or roll a sail on its yard or boom.

gaff The spar on which the head of a "gaff-rigged" fore-and-aft sail is extended; one end has a jaw which fits around the mast.

garboard The plank next to a ship's keel.

gasket A line or band used to lash a furled sail.

glass A telescope or spyglass.

grab A device used for clutching an object.

grego A coarse warm jacket or coat with a hood, formerly worn by seamen.

gunwale The upper edge of a ship's or boat's side.

half hitch A simple knot tied by passing the end of a line around an object, across the main part of the line, and then through the resulting loop.

halyard A rope or tackle for hoisting and lowering yards and sails.

handsomely Slowly and with care; particularly when handling lines which are under strain.

hardtack A saltless, hard biscuit or bread made of flour and water, which keeps for a long time.

hawse Strongly reinforced and lined hole through the hull, above the waterline on the bow, for the passage of the anchor chain or hawser.

hawser A large rope used for towing or mooring a ship.

head A term applied generally to the fore part of a vessel.

headsail A sail set forward of the foremast.

heave To pull strongly on a line or cable, or to raise an anchor; also, the rise and fall of the waves.

heave to To bring a ship to a stop.

helm A lever or wheel controlling the rudder of a ship for steering.

hold Internal cavity of a ship, between the lower deck and floor, where cargo, stores, and ballast are kept.

holystone A soft sandstone used to scrub a ship's decks.

hove See *heave* and *heave to*.

hove in stays Said of a vessel in the act of tacking.

hull The frame or body of a ship exclusive of masts, yards, sails, and rigging.

Jack-stay A bar or wire rope along a yard of a ship to which the sails are fastened.

jaggery An unrefined brown sugar made from palm sap.

japan Any of several varnishes yielding a hard brilliant finish.

jib A triangular sail set on a stay extending from the head of the foremast to the bowsprit or the jib boom.

jib boom A spar extending the bowsprit.

jigger A small fore-and-aft sail rigged out on a mast and boom from the stern of a sailing vessel.

Jonah or *Jonas* Someone whose presence on board is thought to bring ill fortune to a ship.

keel The main and lowest timber extending along the center of the bottom of a ship and forming the basis of the whole structure.

keelson A longitudinal structure running above and fastened to the keel of a ship, which strengthens and stiffens its framework.

ketch A fore-and-aft rigged vessel having a mainmast and a mizzenmast.

kraken A fabulous Scandinavian sea monster.

lash To fasten tightly, usually by tying down with a line or chain.

lead The name given to a conical piece of lead, with a line, called the lead-line, attached to its upper end. It is used to sound the depth at sea.

lee, leeward The side or direction opposite to the wind direction.

leech The vertical edge of a square sail, or the after edge of a fore-and-aft sail.

line A nautical term for a rope.

list A ship is said to *list* when it leans over to one side.

log The ship's journal, also a device for measuring the speed of a vessel through the water.

luff The leading edge of a fore-and-aft sail.

mainsail The principle sail on the mainmast.

manrope A side rope, as on a ship's gangway or ladder, used as a handrail.

masthead The top of a mast.

meridians Imaginary circles on the surface of the earth, passing through both poles, cutting the equator at right angles, and dividing the earth into degrees of longitude.

mizzenmast The mast aft, or next aft of the mainmast.

offing The part of the deep sea seen by the shore; *to keep a good offing* means to keep well off from the land while under sail.

oilskins Partly waterproof workclothes for bad weather, formerly made of canvas saturated in linseed oil.

painter A line used for securing or towing a boat.

point a rope To undo a rope end and taper the inside yarns with a knife, then reweave the outside threads. This is done to avoid fraying.

poop An enclosed structure at the stern of a ship above the main deck, or the highest and aftmost deck of a ship.

port The left side of a ship looking forward from the stern.

purchase A name given to any sort of mechanical power, as a capstan, windlass, tackle, or lever, which increases the force applied to move or raise heavy objects.

quarter The corner which the stern makes with a ship's side.

quarterdeck That part of the upper deck from the mainmast to right aft, or to the poop.

quartermaster A petty officer who attends to the ship's helm, binnacle, signals, and, sometimes, navigation.

rally in To haul in rapidly.

reach A vessel is said to be *on a reach* when she is sailing across the wind.

reckoning The estimation of a vessel's position by the course steered and the distance run.

reef A part of a sail which can be taken in to reduce its size.

rigging The lines and wires of a vessel.

roundly Smartly and swiftly.

royal The mast, sail, or yard located immediately above the topgallant.

rudder A flat piece of metal or wood used to steer a boat, which is attached upright to or near its stern.

sail bending To fasten the sails to their proper yards or stays.

samphire A fleshy European seacoast plant.

schooner A fore-and-aft rigged vessel with two or more masts, whose foremast is usually shorter than the other masts.

scuttle A square opening cut through a vessel's deck or through any of her hatches.

set or *setting of sails* To add more sails to those already employed.

sheet A line or chain that regulates the angle at which a sail is set in relation to the wind. To *sheet home* is to bring a sheet to its proper location.

shroud Part of the standing rigging; lateral supporting lines or wires leading from the mast or masthead to the ship's sides.

simoom A hot, dry, violent, dust-laden wind from Asian and African deserts.

skysail A light sail in a square-rigged vessel that is next above the royal.

slab-line A line used to pull in the slack of the lower sails in order to prevent them from shaking or being split while they are hauled up.

sloop A vessel with one mast, commonly rigged wholly with fore-and-aft sails.

southeaster A wind coming from the southeast.

southwester A wind coming from the southwest.

spanking Brisk, lively.

spar A stout rounded wood or metal piece (as a mast, boom, gaff, or yard) used to support rigging.

spencer A fore-and-aft sail set with a gaff, located behind the foremast or mainmast.

squall A high wind arriving suddenly and ceasing suddenly.

square-rigged ship A ship rigged so that the principal sails are extended on yards fastened to the masts horizontally and at their center.

square sail A four-sided sail.

square the yards To bring a ship's yards to right angles with her keel.

starboard The right side of a ship looking forward from the stern.

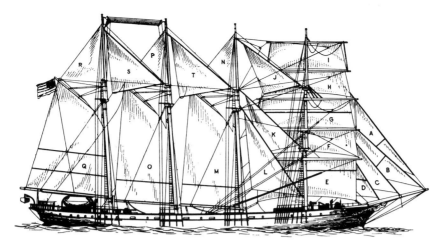

FOUR MASTED BARKENTINE

A–Flying jib
B–Outer jib
C–Jib
D–Fore-topmast staysail
E–Foresail

F–Fore lower topsail
G–Fore upper topsail
H–Fore lower togallant sail
I–Fore upper topgallant sail
J–Main topmast staysail

H–Upper main staysail
L–Main staysail
M–Mainsail
N–Main topsail
O–Mizzen

P–Mizzen topsail
Q–Spanker
R–Spanker topsail
S–Spanker topmast staysail
T–Mizzen topmast staysail

stave off To thrust a boat or a floating object away from a jetty or a ship's side with a spar or boat hook.

stay A large rope used to support a mast.

staysail A triangular sail hoisted on a stay.

steerageway A rate of motion sufficient to make a ship or boat respond to movements of the rudder.

stern The rear end of a boat.

sternpost The principal piece of timber in a vessel's stern frame from which the keel is hung.

stow To load or pack.

strand The shore.

strike To lower or let down a flag, sail, yard, or topmast; also applied to lowering the colors as a token of surrender to an enemy.

studding sail A light quadrilateral sail set outside of any square sail on a boom rigged on a yardarm. Studding sails are carried only in a fair wind in moderate weather.

stun' sail See *studding sail*.

sweeps Large oars used in small sailing vessels.

tack The run of a sailing ship in one direction, or the lower forward corner of a fore-and-aft sail.

tacking Changing the direction of a ship by turning the bow to the wind, and shifting the sails to the opposite side.

tackle Any system of pulleys comprised of a minimum of two blocks.

taffrail The upper part of the stern of a wooden ship.

three-cornered scraper A small, triangular, iron instrument used to scrape the planks of a vessel.

thwart The seats across a row boat, upon which the oarsmen sit.

top A platform across the head of a lower mast.

topgallant The topmost, or third, part of a full-rigged mast. In the older square rig, the topgallant sail was the third from the bottom.

topsail The second sail above the deck on any mast.

transom Any of several transverse beams secured to the sternpost of a boat.

trim The proper disposition of the weight that a boat carries.

to trim To adjust the sails properly for the wind and course.

truck A circular piece of wood fixed on the head of each of a ship's highest masts.

trysail A fore-and-aft sail with a boom and gaff, hoisted on a lower mast. It is sometimes called a *spencer* or *spanker*.

turn To coil a line by passing it around something, or the coils themselves.

turret A revolving armored structure on a warship that protects one or more guns mounted within it.

warp A line used for towing a ship in harbor.

weather bow Bow on the windward side of a vessel.

whipping a rope's ends To secure the end of a rope by wrapping it with twine or wire to avoid fraying.

williwaw A sudden, violent gust of cold land air, common along mountainous coasts of high latitudes.

windlass A horizontal barrel on vertical posts, which is turned by a crank so that a hoisting rope is wound around the barrel.

wear ship To bring a vessel upon the other tack by turning her head around, away from the wind.

yards Long, cylindrical, tapered timbers, which are slung by their center to the mast horizontally. The yards are used for spreading square sails.

yardarms The ends of a yard.

Illustration Captions

Cover illustration: An American clipper ship in the giant seas encountered off Cape Horn. The number of sails set has been greatly reduced in the early stages of a gale. All hands are now out on the lower yards of the foremast attempting to put a secure furl on two more sails.

pages 2 and 3: Warships of the United States Navy sailing for South America in 1858. The squadron was sent to the Rio de la Plata after a fort in Paraguay fired on an American ship during a surveying expedition. War was avoided when Paraguay agreed to pay $10,000 in compensation for the incident.

page 8: a capstan.

pages 10 and 11: New Bedford artist Benjamin Russell produced many scenes showing American whalers at work. In this print, a fleet of whaling ships pursues its prey at the edge of the Arctic ice pack, off the coast of Alaska. One vessel, on the far right, has been abandoned after being trapped in the ice.

page 12: An oarlock.

page 13: Woodcut from Columbus' official report of his first voyage.

page 14: Woodcut of a caravel similar to the *Santa Maria*, from the Basel 1493 edition of Columbus' official report of his first voyage.

page 16: A spool of Manila rope.

pages 18 and 19: The full-rigged ship *Meridian* of New York with her sail shortened down to a single topsail in a rising gale. A wave has already torn loose one of her boats, which is precariously hanging from a davit on the port side.

page 20: The *Spray* is the small sloop in which Captain Slocum sailed single-handedly around the world.

page 22: Hemp rope.

page 24: Whaling ships caught in Arctic Ocean ice, September 1871. In this worst single disaster to hit the American whaling fleet, thirty-four vessels were lost, yet all 1,217 men on board succeeded in crossing the ice to surviving ships in open water.

page 27: Newfoundland-born navigator Bob Bartlett commanded Admiral Peary's ship on the first successful expedition to the North Pole in 1909, and for many years operated his own schooner *Effie M. Morrissey* as an Arctic research vessel.

page 30: A Navy lantern.

page 32: The Playa, Panama.

page 35: Above: Unloading on the beach during low tide at Murray Bay, Quebec.
Below: Cornish fishing fleet landing fish.

page 36: A quadrant

page 39: A group of navigational instruments used on board nineteenth century sailing ships. The barometer on the left, hung in brass gimbals to compensate for the motion of the ship, warned mariners of changes in the weather. The quadrant in the center was used to find the ship's position through astronomical observations. The traverse board on the right was used to keep a record of course changes and distances run, and the telltale compass hung over the captain's bunk so he could keep a check on the course being steered.

page 40: A ship's bell.

pages 42 and 43: Two hand-colored engravings show whaling in southern waters in the first half of the nineteenth century. In the first, a whaleboat has been maneuvered into position for harpooning a giant sperm whale basking on the surface. In the second picture, the whale, apparently now in its death throes, has succeeded in swamping the boat and dumping its occupants into the sea.

page 45: As the number of whales in tropical waters became depleted in the late 1800s, whaling vessels ventured ever deeper into the Arctic. There the whalers obtained ivory walrus tusks that could be scrimshawed in the same way as whale teeth, either by themselves or by Eskimo craftsmen. The subjects of these cribbage boards, and style of the work, suggest that Eskimo craftsmen did this work.

page 46: A sailing ship lying at anchor in the harbor of Puerto Montt, Chile, at the southern end of that country's railway system. In the distance, snow-capped peaks of the Andes tower over Chile's lake district.

page 47: A copy of a painting by the British-born artist J. Pringle, showing the Smith & Dimon Shipyard on New York's East River. In the 1840s this yard produced the first true clipper ships, *Rainbow* and *Sea Witch*. Pringle has recorded the activity in a mid-nineteenth century yard in this view, including the sawing of large planks on far left, to the steaming of planks for bending on far right.

pages 50 and 51: The American transatlantic packet ship *Orpheus*, built at New York in 1833, is shown off the entrance to the Port of Liverpool, where she traded regularly, in this painting by British artist Samuel Walters.

page 52: A reef or square knot.

page 55: A painted chart of the private flags of shipowners and merchants of the Port of New York. These flags identified the vessels of a particular owner at sea, and were flown at the signal station at the entrance to the Port of New York when an owner's ship was sighted returning from a voyage.

page 56: A model of the first *Ambrose Channel* Lightship stationed in 1908 off the new entrance to the Port of New York. The ship herself, modernized in the 1930s, can now be visited by the public at the South Street Seaport Museum in Lower Manhattan, New York.

page 58: This lively whaling tableau is an example of the whaler's art called "scrimshaw," practiced on shipboard in the mid-nineteenth century. In this scene, hand-engraved on a polished sperm whale tooth, the *Ranger* of London is shown backing her sails to stand by her three boats as they pursue a school of whales, some already fatally wounded and some spouting blood.

page 59: Looking toward New York's upper bay on a busy day in the mid–1800s. Governors Island's prominent Fort, Castle Williams, is on the left, and the hills of Staten Island appear in the distance.

page 60: An oak deck bucket.

page 62: In the 1850s, at the height of the clipper ship era, the sailing of a vessel from a major East Coast port was announced on colorful lithographed cards, which were distributed to potential shippers of cargo or agents for passengers.

page 63: New York's East River waterfront at the turn of the century, with the Brooklyn Bridge, completed in 1883, in the background. Coastal steamships and lighter barges of all descriptions crowd the slips between piers jutting out into the river.

page 64: A carrick bend.

pages 66 and 67: The packet ship *Great Western* built at New York in 1851 by William H. Webb was one of the finest sailing passenger vessels on the North Atlantic. On her fore topsail, and the flag at her mainmast, is the symbol of her owners, the Black Ball Line, that pioneered in 1818 scheduled transatlantic service.

page 68: The American clipper ship *Reynard* built at Newburyport, Massachusetts, in 1856, shown by British artist J. Hughes off the Port of Liverpool. The *Reynard* sailed in the trade between San Francisco and Hong Kong, and out of both Boston and New York, and stopped at British ports as well.

page 69: A ship can have many lives. The ocean-going side-wheel steamship *Western Metropolis*, built in Brooklyn, New York, in 1863, first served as a northern troopship in the Civil War. She later carried passengers and cargo between New York and Bremen, Germany.

page 70: A cleat.

pages 74 and 75: American warships under sail off the south coast of England on a friendly visit to the British Naval Base in Portsmouth.

pages 78 and 79: The *Sovereign of the Seas* of 1852, built in Boston and owned in New York, was one of the fastest clipper ships built. She is shown here approaching the New York pilot station off Sandy Hook, flying the red, white, and blue house flag of her owners, Grinnell, Minturn & Company.

page 80: A Spirit compass.

pages 82 and 83: An American clipper ship in the giant seas encountered off Cape Horn. The number of sails set has been greatly reduced in the early stages of a gale. All hands are now out on the lower yards of the foremast attempting to put a secure furl on two more sails.

page 84: Clipper ship cards were imaginatively decorated with a subject or scene referring to the name of the vessel, and were used as advertisements to generate business.

page 87: This clipper ship card advertising the sailing of the *I. F. Chapman*, a full-rigged ship built by her namesake at Thomaston, Maine in 1855, provides an authentic depiction of goods arriving on an open pier along New York City's South Street. The *Chapman* undoubtedly displayed an advertising sail like the one shown, to alert shippers of her destination.

page 90: A ring buoy.

page 92: A portrait doesn't reveal whether a captain was kindhearted and fair or brutal and unjust. This captain, William C. Thompson, commanded packet ships of the Kermit line of New York. He was also involved in early efforts to introduce steamships on the North Atlantic, in the 1840s commanding the iron steamer *Sarah Sands*.

page 95: The New York waterfront at the foot of Maiden Lane in 1828. Packet ships and China traders fill the slips, with their long jib booms extending almost to the opposite sidewalk. Brick counting houses and business establishments served shipping lines at South Street, built on newly completed East River landfill.

page 96: A lifeboat.

pages 101 and 105: Illustrated sheet music from the mid-nineteenth century indicates America's fascination with the hazards of travel by sea. "Man the Lifeboat" shows one of the early surfboats manned by volunteers, which were stationed along particularly dangerous stretches of coastline. A sailor could remain at sea for more than two years, and many songs expressed the loneliness of his sweetheart waiting at home.

pages 110 and 111: Vessels anchored off of Hong Kong in the mid-1800s.

page 112: An American foghorn.

page 114: A Scandinavian bark leaving port. She is fitted with a windmill forward of the mizzenmast to pump out water seeping in through the seams of her wooden hull.

page 116: A heavy galvanized pail.

page 118: The steamship depicted on "God Preserve the Mariner" is based on the early transatlantic passenger vessel, the *President*, that vanished on a voyage in 1841.

page 122: A coiled Manila rope.

page 125: Shipping in the Elbe River at Hamburg, Germany, early in this century. A passenger launch churns past a moored freighter and sailing ship, followed in the distance by a steam tugboat.

pages 130 and 131: Some of the finest American side-wheel steamboats were built for the Hudson River, where in 1807 Robert Fulton had his first success with a steam-powered vessel. When completed in 1880, the *Albany* was the largest and most modern of the day boats running between New York City and her namesake city. She carried passengers until 1948, and in the last years was an excursion boat on the Potomac River.

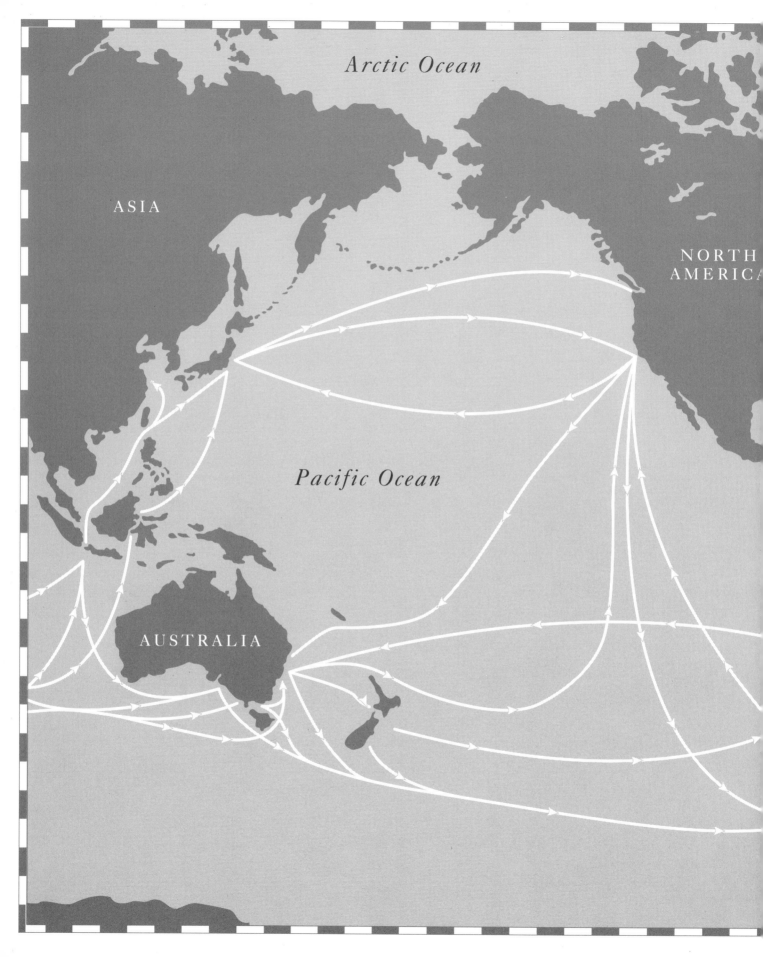